Sue Hackman | **Alan Howe** | **Patrick Scott**

Hodder English Starters: Sentence Level

SENTENCE LEVEL

Hodder & Stoughton

A MEMBER OF THE HODDER HEADLINE GROUP

ACKNOWLEDGEMENTS

The author and publishers would like to thank the following contributors:

Paul Evans	• Sections	A Starting sentences B Asides and extras
John Williams	• Sections	C Clarifying ambiguity H Pace and punch I Standard English
Sonya Austin	• Sections	D Time and motion E Speech
Karyn Taylor	• Sections	F Paragraphs G The shape of writing J Other types of non-fiction

Copyright Text:
pp136 & 137 *The Other Facts of Life* © Morris Gleitzman, 1985, Puffin; pp138, 139 & 158 *Stormbreaker* © 2000 Anthony Horowitz.
Reproduced by permission of the publisher Walker Books Ltd., London; p157 *The Snake-stone* by Berlie Doherty; p157 *Collision Course* by
Nigel Hinton; p158 *Burning Up* by Caroline B. Cooney; p158 *Throwaways* by Ian Strachan; p158 *Dear Nobody* by Berlie Doherty; p174
(book blurb), p175 (travel through time…), p178 (Jean Marie Le Bris… & The world's first…) & p179 (The invention of copper… & Fire
engines…) from *Travel Through Time* by Susan Myars and Colin H Payne; p185 *The Lives of Christopher Chant* by Diane Wynne Jones;
p185 *The Ceremony* by Martyn Corpus.

Artwork on p128 by Philip Page.

Orders: please contact Bookpoint Ltd, 130 Milton Park, Abingdon, Oxon OX14 4SB. Telephone: (44) 01235 827720,
Fax: (44) 01235 400454.
Lines are open from 9.00am - 6.00pm, Monday to Saturday, with a 24 hour message answering service.
Email address: orders@bookpoint.co.uk

British Library Cataloguing in Publication Data
A catalogue record for this title is available from The British Library

ISBN 0 340 79119 5

First published 2001
Impression number   10 9 8 7 6 5 4 3 2
Year   2005 2004 2003 2002 2001

Cover photo from Photodisc.
Typeset by Lorraine Inglis.
Printed in Great Britain for Hodder & Stoughton Educational, a division of Hodder Headline Plc, 338 Euston Road, London NW1 3BH
by Hobbs the Printers, Totton, Hampshire.

Contents

KS3 English Framework objectives

This grid shows which KS3 English Framework Objectives for Year 7 are covered in each starter activity.

STARTER ACTIVITY	KS3 OBJECTIVES (YEAR 7)
A. Starting sentences	
1. Different ways of starting sentences	Sn 1 Subordinate clauses
	Sn 3 Boundary punctuation
2. Starting with a concession	Sn 1 Subordinate clauses
	Sn 3 Boundary punctuation
3. Starting with a reason	Sn 1 Subordinate clauses
4. Subordinators	Sn 1 Subordinate clauses
5. Starting with 'Being'	Sn 1 Subordinate clauses
	Sn 3 Boundary punctuation
6. Starting with other -ing verbs	Sn 1 Subordinate clauses
	Sn 3 Boundary punctuation
7. Starting with place	Sn 1 Subordinate clauses
	Sn 3 Boundary punctuation
8. Starting with time	Sn 1 Subordinate clauses
9. Different ways of starting the same sentence 1	Sn 1 Subordinate clauses
	Sn 3 Boundary punctuation
10. Different ways of starting the same sentence 2	Sn 1 Subordinate clauses
	Sn 3 Boundary punctuation
B. Asides and extras	
1. Expanding nouns 1	Sn 2 Noun phrases
2. Expanding nouns 2	Sn 2 Noun phrases
3. Expanding verbs	Extends Sn 2 Noun phrases
4. Dropping an extra clause into a sentence	Sn 1 Subordinate clauses
	Sn 3 Boundary punctuation
5. Comma splicing	Sn 1 Subordinate clauses
	Sn 3 Boundary punctuation
6. Commas	Sn 3 Boundary punctuation
7. The complex sentence	Sn 1 Subordinate clauses
	Sn 3 Boundary punctuation
8. Revision	Sn 1 Subordinate clauses
	Sn 3 Boundary punctuation
C. Clarifying meaning	
1. Ambiguity 1	Sn 6 Resolve ambiguity
2. Ambiguity 2	Sn 6 Resolve ambiguity
3. The problem with pronouns	Sn 6 Resolve ambiguity
4. Resolving ambiguity by sensible sequencing	Sn 6 Resolve ambiguity
5. Passives	Sn 5 Active or passive voice
6. Hiding the agent	Sn 5 Active or passive voice
7. Laying the blame	Sn 5 Active or passive voice
8. Actives, passives and agents	Sn 5 Active or passive voice

STARTER ACTIVITY	KS3 OBJECTIVES (YEAR 7)
D. Time and motion	
1. Tenses 1	Sn 4 Tense management
2. Tenses 2	Sn 4 Tense management
3. Auxiliary verbs	Sn 4 Tense management
	Wd 17 Word classes
4. Verb phrases	Sn 4 Tense management
	Wd 17 Word classes
5. Lonely verbs	Sn 4 Tense management
	Wd 17 Word classes
6. Irregular verbs 1	Sn 4 Tense management
7. Irregular verbs 2	Sn 4 Tense management
8. Irregular verbs 3	Sn 4 Tense management
9. Changing tenses	Sn 4 Tense management
10. Prevailing tenses	Sn 4 Tense management
E. Speech	
1. Ground rules	Sn 7 Speech punctuation
2. Commas – where exactly do they go?	Sn 3 Boundary punctuation
	Sn 7 Speech punctuation
3. The speaker tag	Sn 3 Boundary punctuation
	Sn 7 Speech punctuation
4. Paragraphing dialogue	Sn 8 Starting paragraphs
5. Dialogue	Sn 8 Starting paragraphs
	Sn 18 Sentences in older text
6. Alternatives to 'exclaimed'	Wd 14 Word meaning in context
7. Alternatives to 'asked'	Wd 14 Word meaning in context
8. Alternatives to 'said'	Wd 14 Word meaning in context
F. Paragraphs	
1. Cues to start a new paragraph 1	Sn 8 Starting paragraphs
2. Cues to start a new paragraph 2	Sn 8 Starting paragraphs
3. Paragraph structure 1	Sn 9 Main point of paragraph
	Sn 10 Paragraph structure
	R 7 Identify main ideas
4. Paragraph structure 2	Sn 9 Main point of paragraph
	Sn 10 Paragraph structure
	R 7 Identify main ideas
5. Paragraph structure 3	Sn 9 Main point of paragraph
	Sn 10 Paragraph structure
	R 7 Identify main ideas
6. Paragraph structure 4	Sn 9 Main point of paragraph
	Sn 10 Paragraph structure
	R 7 Identify main ideas
7. Paragraph diagrams 1	Sn 9 Main point of paragraph
	Sn 10 Paragraph structure
	R 3 Compare presentation
8. Paragraph diagrams 2	Sn 9 Main point of paragraph
	Sn 10 Paragraph structure
	R 3 Compare presentation

STARTER ACTIVITY	KS3 OBJECTIVES (YEAR 7)
9. Paragraph diagrams 3	Sn 10 Paragraph Structure
	R 3 Compare presentation
10. Paragraph composition 1	Sn 12 Sequencing paragraphs
	Wd 20 Connectives
11. Paragraph composition 2	Sn 12 Sequencing paragraphs
	Wd 20 Connectives
12. Paragraph organisation	Sn 8 Starting paragraphs
	Sn 9 Main point of paragraph
	Sn 12 Sequencing paragraphs
13. Paragraph links and signposts 1	Sn 6 Resolve ambiguity
	Sn 11 Sentence variety
	Sn 12 Sequencing paragraphs
14. Paragraph links and signposts 2	Sn 12 Sequencing paragraphs
	Wd 20 Connectives
15. Paragraph links and signposts 3	Sn 12 Sequencing paragraphs
	Wd 20 Connectives
16. Key sentences	Sn 8 Starting paragraphs
	Sn 9 Main point of paragraph
	R 7 Identify main ideas
17. Grabbing the reader's attention in the first line	Sn 8 Starting paragraphs
	Sn 9 Main point of paragraph
18. Punchline conclusions 1	Sn 11 Sentence variety
	Sn 12 Sequencing paragraphs
19. Punchline conclusions 2	Sn 11 Sentence variety
	Sn 12 Sequencing paragraphs

G. The shape of writing

1. Signposts	Sn 12 Sequencing paragraphs
	Sn 13a Information
	Wd 20 Connectives
	Wr 10 Organise texts appropriately
2. Layout	Sn 13 Stylistic conventions of non-fiction
	Wr 10 Organise texts appropriately
3. Organising argument 1	Sn 10 Paragraph structure
	Sn 13e Persuasion
	Wr 10 Organise texts appropriately
	Wr 15 Express a view
4. Organising argument 2	Sn 10 Paragraph structure
	Sn 13e Persuasion
	Wr 10 Organise texts appropriately
	Wr 15 Express a view
5. Organising information	Sn 10 Paragraph structure
	Sn 13a Information
	Wr 10 Organise texts appropriately
	Wr 11 Present information
6. Comparison and contrast 1	Sn 10 Paragraph structure
	Sn 13f Discursive writing
	Wr 10 Organise texts appropriately

STARTER ACTIVITY	KS3 OBJECTIVES (YEAR 7)
7. Comparison and contrast 2	Sn 10 Paragraph structure
	Sn 13f Discursive writing
	Wr 10 Organise texts appropriately

H. Pace and punch

STARTER ACTIVITY	KS3 OBJECTIVES (YEAR 7)
1. Short breathless sentences	Sn 11 Sentence variety
2. Tension	Sn 11 Sentence variety
3. Long and easy sentences 1	Sn 11 Sentence variety
4. Long and easy sentences 2	Sn 11 Sentence variety
5. Leaving the best till last	Sn 11 Sentence variety
	Sn 12 Sequencing paragraphs
6. Paragraph endings 1	Sn 12 Sequencing paragraphs
7. Paragraph endings 2	Sn 12 Sequencing paragraphs
8. Paragraph rhythm 1	Sn 11 Sentence variety
9. Paragraph rhythm 2	Sn 11 Sentence variety

I. Standard English

STARTER ACTIVITY	KS3 OBJECTIVES (YEAR 7)
1. Great things about writing	Sn 16 Speech and writing
	Sn 17 Standard English
2. Great things about speech	Sn 16 Speech and writing
3. Appropriateness in speech and writing 1	Sn 16 Speech and writing
	Sn 17 Standard English
4. Appropriateness in speech and writing 2	Sn 16 Speech and writing
	Sn 17 Standard English
5. Agreement	Sn 4 Tense management
	Sn 17 Standard English
6. Formality 1	Sn 15 Vary formality
7. Formality 2	Sn 15 Vary formality
	Sn 17 Standard English
8. Formality 3	Sn 15 Vary formality

J. Other types of non-fiction

STARTER ACTIVITY	KS3 OBJECTIVES (YEAR 7)
1. Text types 1	Sn 13 Stylistic conventions of non-fiction
2. Text types 2	Sn 13 Stylistic conventions of non-fiction
3. Text types 3	Sn 13 Stylistic conventions of non-fiction
4. Text types 4	Sn 13 Stylistic conventions of non-fiction
5. Giving directions	Sn 13d Instructions
	Wr 13 Instructions and directions
6. Instructions	Sn 13d Instructions
	Wr 13 Instructions and directions
7. Explanation	Sn 13c Explanation
	Wr 12 Develop logic
8. Recount	Sn 13b Recount
9. Persuasion	Sn 13e Persuasion
	Wr 15 Express a view
10. Analysis	Sn 14 Subject conventions

About starters

Like all the best ideas, starters are nothing new. Effective teachers have always known that a fast and focused start creates a positive atmosphere for learning, and gets the lesson off to a flying start. Starters give a sense of quick gains early in the lesson and this builds pupils' confidence. They also help to break the lesson into manageable spans, so that attention can be caught, developed and then re-captured with a shift of focus.

Typically, a starter might last around 10-15 minutes depending on the length of the whole lesson, and focus on one idea. Its speed and focus lends itself to 'spotlighting' key ideas or conventions, and thus to direct teaching.

Active learning

Starters are not a passive learning experience. That would undermine the idea of an engaging start. Most of the starters are posed as problem-solving activities or investigations, and pupils are drawn in to investigate and solve the challenges posed by the starters. All of the starters are organised as whole class activities, and there is a high premium on oral, interactive and participatory work. Most of them feature short bursts of work in pairs or groups, particularly where investigative thinking is required. Pupils are expected to consider what they already know and generalise from it. The idea is to spark off thinking by drawing out latent knowledge for exploration.

Teaching starters

Starters do not claim to be exhaustive teaching, even though they are explicit in nature. It is for the teacher to apply and secure them in practice. In reading lessons, attention can be drawn to the use of sentence techniques studied in recent starter sessions deployed to good effect in context. Pupils will come to texts more experienced in analysis and better able to explain how effects are achieved. In shared writing, the class will be better able to discuss and compare different ways of expressing ideas for maximum effect.

The pace of teaching is cracking. Starters depend on focus and challenge. At first, teachers over-run because the prevailing teaching style in secondary schools is geared to exposition and follow-up consolidation in context. This is the kind of teaching that aims to anchor learning by in-depth treatment in context.

Starters operate on a slightly different (but not mutually exclusive) premise that you can teach explicitly and rapidly and then consolidate in two ways: firstly, by revisiting 'little and often', and secondly by highlighting the techniques studied when the class reads and writes longer text.

The benefit of doing it this way is that it allows you to deal with skills, conventions and techniques in passing with a lightness of touch when you teach reading and writing. We do a disservice to literature if we try to spin off it every aspects of language teaching: it can be both spurious and frustrating for the reader. And anyway, we can't be sure that all the things we need to teach will be covered if we wait for naturally-occurring opportunities.

The content of starter sessions

The use of starters ensures the systematic coverage of objectives, and releases us from ruining texts by having to teach these things from first principles every time we come across them.

The starters address the sentence-level objectives in the Framework of Objectives for English in Year 7. If the pupils have been taught the National Literacy Strategy in Year 6, they may well have come across some of the terms and ideas.

Issues

Resourcing

This book provides step-by-step teaching plans and OHT masters for almost a hundred starters. A number of starters also include photocopy word cards or sheets when an investigation is too large to fit on an OHT. It is probably worth the effort of laminating the cards to keep for further use.

Pupils' own work is a rich source of starter material. If you plan ahead, you can keep an eye open for effective sentences in pupils' work to exemplify the point of the starter, or so demonstrate how a starter you have used has been effectively applied in context.

Another valuable resource is a collection of hand-held mini-whiteboards so that pupils can have a go at the sentence structures taught. They love the impermanence of the whiteboard: it holds no threats. Cheap and compact whiteboards can be created by laminating A4 white card.

Differentiation

Starters work well with the less able because they are engaging and short and also because they yield clear learning points. The able like them for much the same reasons: they see them as challenging, pressurised and explicit. Most starters work well in a mixed ability setting, but there is absolutely no point in doing a starter if the pupils already have the rule or topic under control.

There are built-in supports for differentiation in a typical starter activity, because a typical sequence poses incremental challenges:

▶ Identifying patterns – the vast majority of pupils should be able to do this
▶ Generalising about patterns – the majority of pupils should be able to do this
▶ Explaining patterns and conventions – many pupils will be able to do this
▶ Finding and rationalising exceptions – some pupils will be able to do this
▶ Extending or speculating about a pattern – a few pupils will be able to do this.

The challenge lies in the pressure to articulate and to explain, and then to apply effectively.

Managing answers

Since starters are interactive and direct, there is a premium on the ability to manage discussion. The whole-class approach means that one has to be quite careful to create a climate in which mistakes are tolerated and construed as learning opportunities.

There is a tricky moment when you receive an incorrect answer. You want to value the effort but you also want to remedy the misconception. In general, it is best to tackle misconceptions as a whole class matter, and not to single out the pupil who made the error. The problem can be avoided if the starter is treated as a short investigation into which a range of solutions can be suggested and then tested. At least one good reason for doing it this way is that it mirrors the real-life working process of clever thinkers. Never dodge. If it's wrong, say so, but follow up with a constructive comment.

Assessment

Starters offer instant assessment. You get immediate feedback on the success of your teaching, and you don't store up time-consuming marking. A classroom assistant can be well-used at the front of the class, noting the responses of pupils, and perhaps returning to the topic later with a smaller group.

Fun

It is hardly fashionable to say so, but starters are also good because they are fun. Boys in particular warm to the oral and direct approach. And if they are not fun, the worst they can be is brief and businesslike. It is not dreary to be direct: it can make life easier. But don't wait to be persuaded: try them and see. Starters will sell themselves to you because they work.

Sue Hackman

Section A: Starting sentences

A1 Different ways of starting sentences

AIM: To introduce the idea of starting a sentence with a subordinate clause

YOU WILL NEED:

▶ OHT A1.1

1 Show the first sentence on OHT A1.1 and establish some key terms.

2 Explain that a **clause** is a mini-sentence that makes sense on its own. Many sentences have just one clause but others join together two or three. This sentence has two.

3 Explain that the **main clause** in this sentence is 'I stayed up' because it makes sense on its own.

4 Explain that 'even though I was tired' is a **subordinate clause** because it can't stand on its own and depends on the main clause for its meaning. They have to be read together to make sense.

5 Underline 'even though' and point out that these words warn you that a subordinate clause is about to follow. 'Even though' tells you it is just an aside to the main point. It is known as a **subordinator**.

6 Now show the second sentence. The main clause 'I stayed up' has moved but it is still the main clause – it makes sense on its own. Likewise, 'even though I was tired' is still the subordinate clause.

7 Point out the comma. The rule is that you put a comma between the main and subordinate clause if you move the subordinate clause earlier in the sentence.

8 Point out that most school writing suffers from being expressed in the way the first sentence is expressed. To sound more sophisticated and to vary expression, pupils should try to be more confident about moving the position of the subordinate clause.

9 Now reveal the other sentences on the OHT and cover only the first sentence.

10 Ask pupils to identify the main clause in each case. This will reveal that all the sentences start with a subordinate clause.

11 Ask pupils to pick out the subordinators. This will reveal that all the sentences start with a subordinator.

12 Also note that all the sentences use a comma. Read some aloud to illustrate how easy it is to hear where the commas should go, as well as working it out by clauses.

13 Now ask pairs to choose a sentence and imitate it, using the same subordinator and structure but with new content. For example:

> Even though I was tired, I stayed up.
>
> Even though Sam was late, we waited for him
>
> Even though we were hungry, we ate little.

14 Take examples from each sentence and reward effective sentences.

A2 Starting with a concession

AIM:	To introduce the idea of starting a sentence with a subordinate clause of concession

YOU WILL NEED:
▶ OHT A2.1

1 Ask pupils if they ever hear a word and know before the sentence is finished that the person is going to express a reservation? For example, Even though … Look for the responses: despite, unless, however, but, except, even though, unfortunately, etc.

2 Show OHT A2.1. Demonstrate that 'I went out' is the main clause by covering up the first half to show how 'I went out' makes sense on its own. Then cover up the second half to show how 'Although it was raining' can't make full sense on its own. It needs the main clause to make sense.

Note: there are two clauses in this sentence: the main clause ('I went out') which can stand on its own two feet and could be expressed as a sentence in its own right. The other clause is the subordinate clause because it depends on the main clause for its meaning. It begins with a subordinating conjunction. The very word 'although' warns you that this is a subordinate clause.

3 Point out the word 'Although'. The first word of the sentence is one of those words you generated at the beginning to express a reservation or make a concession. Pose the question: when someone says 'although' you already know what comes next. What are they going to say? Look for the response: they are going to qualify or concede something.

4 Point out the comma. When the subordinate clause comes first in the sentence, it is usually separated from the main clause by a comma.

5 Reveal the rest of the OHT and ask for volunteers to suggest different ways of completing the other sentences.

A3 Starting with a reason

AIM:	To introduce the idea of starting a sentence with a subordinate clause of reason

YOU WILL NEED:
▶ OHT A3.1

1   Look at the first sentence on OHT A3.1 and refer back to your discussion of subordinate clauses in the previous starter. Ask pupils to identify the main clause ('Jenny went on ahead') and the subordinate clause ('Because John was scared'). Point out the comma which marks the boundary between the main and subordinate clause.

2   Underline the word 'Because' and point out how it warns the reader that what is coming is a reason.

3   Now ask pupils what other words would go here and still mean 'because' (i.e. give a reason for Jenny going ahead). Look for the responses: as, since.

4   Invite pupils in pairs to make up similar sentences beginning with 'because', 'as' or 'since'.

5   Allow 2 minutes, and ask them to check on three things: that they have a main clause as well as a subordinate clause, and a comma between them.

6   Take an example to write up on the OHT. If it lacks a subordinate clause, ask the class to provide one before you write. Leave out the comma, but ask who in the class could come up and put it in the right place. Follow up by asking someone to explain why it belongs there.

7   Ask a few more to speak their sentences aloud and check with the class that each sentence makes complete sense.

A4 Subordinators

AIM:	To generate a list of useful subordinators for sentence construction

YOU WILL NEED:
▶   A4.1 cut up into cards, enough sets for one between three

1   Remind the class that you have already seen how sentences can start with a subordinate clause that gives a reason or a concession. There are many other types of subordinate clause that can be used. The trick is knowing the words which start such clauses.

2 Distribute the cards on A4.1 between threes and ask them to pick out the large cards first and lay them in a line at the top of the table. Underneath these cards they must sort the small cards. Allow 5 minutes.

3 Take feedback on the TIME group:

after, as, before, since, till, until, when, while, once, whenever.

4 Take the three words 'since', 'as' and 'while' and tell pupils that these words could just have easily been placed in different columns. Ask them to identify which ones. Look for the response:

- while – contrast
- since – reason
- as – reason

5 Draw attention to the blank cards and tell pupils that many of the words could belong in more than one column. The blanks are there to duplicate such words.

- Place: where, wherever
- On condition: if, unless, in case, as long as, supposing
- Reservation or concession: although, though, if, even if, whereas, despite
- Contrast or comparison: whereas, while, whilst, as, like, as if, as though
- Exception: except for, but for
- Reason or purpose: because, since, for, as, to, in order to, so as to, so, so that.

A5 Starting with 'Being'

AIM:	To illustrate how sentences can be varied by starting with a non-finite verb

YOU WILL NEED:
▶ OHT A5.1

1 Have OHT A5.1 ready but covered: this starter involves moving the cover down at each step to reveal a new sentence.

2 Reveal the first sentence: 'John was tired and went to sleep'.
Explain that the word 'and' makes the sentence rather boring. It could be made into a complex sentence beginning with the word 'because'. Ask if anyone can suggest how we might do that.

3 Take ideas and also show the next two sentences on the OHT.

4 Now explain that there is another way of doing it, still creating a complex sentence, but without using a conjunction.

5 Reveal the fourth sentence on the OHT and ask: Can anyone tell me what's missing from that sentence? Look for the response: a comma, and draw out that a comma is needed here between the subordinate clause 'being tired' and the main clause 'John went to sleep'. Show the next sentence which is the correct version.

6 Underline the word 'tired', and ask if they could substitute a different word and still make sense? E.g. exhausted, bored, lazy, overworked, drunk, alone, old.

7 Emphasise to pupils how useful this device is for starting sentences, because it can be combined with a huge number of different words. Then ask: If I asked you to make a sentence about John being scared and hiding under the bed, how would the sentence look? Then show the final sentence as an example.

8 If there is time, invite pupils to make up similar sentences, using the same construction and starting with -ing. Take suggestions. Ask occasionally where the comma would go and why.

A6 Starting with other -ing verbs

AIM:	To introduce a range of other non-finite verbs for starting sentences

YOU WILL NEED:
▶ OHT 6.1

1 Have the OHT ready but covered: this starter involves moving the cover down at each step to reveal a new sentence.

2 Reveal the first sentence and point out the way it starts with a verb ending in -ing. Ask pupils to give you more verbs ending in -ing.

3 Ask pupils to give you a new sentence starting with one of these new verbs, borrowing the structure of the first sentence on the OHT. Listen to some examples.

4 Reveal the second sentence on the OHT and ask pupils where the comma should go. If they give the incorrect answer 'after *warily*', read the sentence aloud and ask them to listen for the shift from one clause to another. Most people can hear it. Go on to identify the main clause ('Jenny crept down the corridor') which is self-standing and the subordinate clause ('Looking warily from side to side') which is dependent on the main clause for its meaning.

5 Move on to consider why we need this kind of sentence. Act out coming in through the door and smiling. Then show the third sentence on the OHT. This is a very effective way of combining two actions in one sentence.

6 Invite someone to come out and demonstrate two simple actions, then ask the class to construct a sentence starting with an -ing verb to yoke the two actions together.

7 Show the fourth and fifth sentences and ask pupils to jot down possible sentences in rough. Share and compare answers. Point out that such sentences have a sophisticated ring and pupils should try to use them occasionally in their work.

A7 Starting with place

AIM:	To suggest how sentences may be started with a prepositional phrase of place

YOU WILL NEED:
▶ OHT A7.1

1 Show the sentences in the upper half of OHT A7.1 and ask pupils to comment on similarities in the way they start. Look for the responses:
- They all start with a mention of setting
- They all start with a preposition
- They all have a comma before the main clause

2 Show the lower half of the OHT and ask the class what the difference in effect would be if the sentences were reversed so that the main clause came first. Look for the response: The upper sentence focuses on Karim, and the lower sentence emphasises the cave. When you change scene in a story, it is often a good idea to introduce the new place at the start of a sentence.

3 Highlight the first words in the upper three sentences and point out that they are all prepositions which indicate place. Challenge the class in groups to come up with as many more as they can think of in one minute.

4 Take responses and list on the board or OHT: on; inside; within; outside; by; near; beyond; among; below; beneath; to; towards; from; into; out of; off; onto; along; down; past; round; throughout.

5 Pick out a few people and ask them to start a sentence with a preposition on the list.

A8 Starting with time

AIM:	To suggest how sentences might be started with a prepositional phrase of time

YOU WILL NEED:
► OHT A7.1

1 Remind pupils that in the last starter, they looked at sentences that started with prepositions of *place*. Today, they are going to look at prepositions of *time*.

2 Show the top half of OHT A7.1 again, and ask pupils if they could replace the first preposition with a different preposition that tells you <u>when</u> it happened. For example:

- Before entering the cave, Karim hesitated. (The new preposition is substituted)
- Meanwhile over in the garage, Phil was arguing with Jenny. (The new preposition is added)
- Already, the rats were gathering in the sewers. (An existing preposition has been moved to the front of the sentence)

3 Write up on the board or OHT the three new prepositions that have been introduced and challenge the class to race to compile a list of prepositions of time. Allow one minute.

4 Take feedback. The list might include: before, during, after, earlier, later, since, meanwhile, whenever, at (e.g. at 4 o'clock), in (e.g. in two hours), on (e.g. on Thursday), for (e.g. for 30 minutes), by (e.g. by the time the bell goes), till, until, now.

5 Now ask pairs of pupils to think of an intriguing sentence to start a story. The sentence must begin with a preposition of time. Start them off with: *During the whole of that term, John Smith lived in fear.*

A9 Different ways of starting the same sentence 1

AIM:	To recognise how easy it is to reposition the prepositional phrase in a sentence

YOU WILL NEED:
► OHT A9.1

1 Have the OHT ready but covered: this starter involves moving the cover down at each step to reveal a new sentence.

2 Reveal the first sentence and pose the question: How many different ways do you think the words of this sentence can be moved around and still make sense?

3 Take suggestions and then show the other two sentences. Point out:
- That the second sentence now starts with a preposition of place like the ones studied in starter A7.
- That the phrase 'in his cell' moves around: the rest stays where it is.

4 Pose the question: Two of these sentences have the same focus, but one is different. Which one and why? Look for the response: the first two are alike, the third is the odd one out.

NB. The first two answer the question: Where was the prisoner crying? The third one answers the question: Which prisoner was crying? In the first two sentences, the phrase is attached to the verb – it tells you more about the crying. It is an adverbial phrase. In the third sentence, it is attached to the prisoner – it is an adjectival phrase.

5 Now try the same thing with the sentence in the middle of the OHT: 'The thief was creeping along the road.' Pose the questions: What are the other two possible sentences? Which one means something different from the other two?

6 Now reveal the final section of the OHT and ask pupils to imagine that they are beginning to write a story. They must work out all the possible sentences which one could make from the phrases provided. Remind them about commas and best effect.

7 Take a range of suggestions, rewarding effective sentences.

8 Continue this idea in the next starter, A10.

A10 Different ways of starting the same sentence 2

AIM:	To recognise how easy it is to reposition the prepositional phrase in a sentence

YOU WILL NEED:
▶ OHT A10.1

1 Show the two clauses at the top of OHT A10.1 and ask pupils how many different ways they can suggest for putting the two clauses into a sentence. Allow less than a minute.

2 Take answers, using the middle section of the OHT as an exemplar if necessary.

3 Draw attention to the commas. Notice how the commas are used to separate the subordinate and main clauses. Ask: Why is there no comma in the second sentence? Look for the response: Commas are only needed if the subordinate clause is moved forward in the sentence. It isn't needed if it comes at the end.

4 Reveal the final section of the OHT. Ask pupils to think of as many ways as possible of putting those three clauses into one sentence.

5 Ask pupils which of their versions has the most sinister effect. This occurs when the main clause is deferred to the end.

6 Take suggestions and write them up, asking in particular where the comma should go.

B1 Expanding nouns 1

AIM: To highlight several ways of expanding a noun with adjectives

YOU WILL NEED:
▶ OHT B1.1
▶ OHT B1.2

1 Remind pupils that one of the earliest and simplest things we learn about enhancing writing is to add adjectives. Ask them to remind you of the function of adjectives: to add information, or detail, about the noun.

2 Look at the first sentence on OHT B1.1, but keep the rest covered. It's a pretty boring sentence. Ask pupils to pick out the two nouns to which we can add adjectives. Ask them to suggest possibilities.

3 Now reveal sentence 2 . Better than the first? No. Why not? Two reasons: too many adjectives and they are repetitious.

4 Tell pupils that larding work with adjectives does not necessarily make it more interesting.

5 Ask pupils if adjectives always come before their noun as they did here? Prompt someone to give you an example of an adjective coming after a noun. Show the third sentence as an example.

6 Swiftly move on to show the fourth sentence. Raise the question of whether one needs to mention that Jenny was angry and upset, if one describes her as *storming* out of the room? It is very often more effective to describe what characters do and say, rather than telling the reader outright what to think.

7 Ask pupils if they can think of another way this sentence could be organised, using the same words but in a different order. Use sentence 5 to illustrate the answer if no-one gets it.

8 Now look at the final sentence. Now you've got the reader guessing! The adjective 'brief' is loaded with suggestion.

9 Show the first sentence on OHT B1.2 and tell pupils they have one minute in pairs to come up with a version in which adjectives have been deployed and the order improved. Listen to three or four contributions, praising effective ideas.

10 Now look at the second sentence on the OHT and ask pupils to replace the boring overused adjectives and improve the sentence construction to make a more interesting paragraph. Allow two minutes then take ideas, praising effective versions.

B2 Expanding nouns 2

AIM: To highlight how nouns can be expanded using prepositional phrases

YOU WILL NEED:
▶ OHT B2.1

1 Remind pupils about the last starter in which they considered how nouns can be enhanced by adjectives. Explain that there is another way in which nouns can be modified.

2 Show the first sentence on the OHT B2.1 The boy is described through a phrase ('in the ragged jumper') which follows the noun. Explain to pupils that they can always use a phrase like this instead of adjectives, by following the noun with a preposition. Underline 'in' and ask pupils to give you more examples of prepositions, e.g. on, across, at, by, with, under, etc.

3 Now ask the class to translate this boy into different story genres. Suppose that the sentence was the first in a horror story: what sort of phrase might set up the appropriate expectations? (e.g. with the eerie smile, in the metal pod). Ask the class for ideas.

4 Now allow pupils time, in pairs, to generate similar versions of the sentence suitable for the stories listed on the lower section of the OHT.

5 Hear some of the examples, praising effective sentences. You may get plausible suggestions even if they don't use prepositions (e.g. The boy holding the alien pod). Comment positively and point out that it's been done without a preposition.

B3 Expanding verbs

AIM: To highlight how you can extend a verb using an adverb or adverbial phrase

YOU WILL NEED:
▶ OHT B3.1

1 Explain that just as you have expanded nouns with adjectives and phrases, so you can expand verbs with adverbs and adverbial phrases. Look at the first sentence on the OHT. Use the second sentence to show how you can expand the verb with an adverb. Then quickly move on to the third sentence to show how you can expand the verb with an adverbial phrase.

2 Now ask pupils to work on the fourth sentence with a partner to suggest an adverb and an adverbial phrase which would make the sentence more effective as the opening to a suspense story. Take suggestions.

3 Look at the fifth sentence and ask pupils to show you every point in that sentence where words or phrases could be added. Use the sixth sentence to confirm answers.

4 Ask pupils to think of words and phrases which could fit in each of those places.

5 You could end up with a sentence like the seventh. A little too much? Take some of the words out to create a more striking effect.

6 Now ask pupils to repeat the final activity using the last sentence. Allow a minute or so and take feedback, rewarding effective sentences.

B4 Dropping an extra clause into a sentence

AIM: To illustrate how to embed a subordinate clause in a sentence

YOU WILL NEED:
▶ OHT B4.1 cut into transparent cards
▶ The lower section of B4.1 cut into paper cards, enough for one set between two.

1 Cut up the words and phrases on OHT B4.1 so that you have OHT word cards to use.

2 On the OHT arrange these words into the sentence: 'Jenny entered the room.'

3 Explain that you want to add an extra clause into this sentence and lay the phrase 'although she was scared' just below the sentence. Ask pupils where it might go. It could, in fact, go at the beginning, end or in the middle.

4 Focus pupils' attention on placing it in the middle. Establish where it would go (after 'Jenny') and then ask what punctuation would be necessary and why. You could ask them to say the sentence aloud slowly, to hear the shift of tone when you drop in an aside.

5 Tell pupils the rule: when you drop extra clauses into the middle (or at the front) of sentences, you must put commas between it and the main clause. Use the transparency commas to do this.

6 Clear the OHT so that you are back with the original sentence and the two commas waiting below it. Introduce the alternative clause: 'who was shaking with fear'. Ask where this can go. Unlike the previous clause, this can only go after 'Jenny'. Ask someone to come and arrange the new sentence:
Jenny, although she was scared, entered the room.

7 Repeat with 'feeling full of confidence', which can go at the beginning middle or end, but once again, focus on the middle position.

8 Distribute the cards made from the lower half of B4.1 and ask pupils to arrange three different sentences.

9 Take feedback then ask who could suggest two sentences in which the extra clause goes at the beginning and how it would be punctuated. Use your own OHT cards to illustrate this:

Although he knew he should stay, John ran off.
Fearing the worst, John ran off.

Note the comma and refer back to the rule introduced earlier.

B5 Comma splicing

> **AIM**: To explain the problem of comma splicing and suggest some ways to avoid it

YOU WILL NEED:
▶ OHT B5.1

1 Show OHT B5.1 and allow them 2 minutes to decide what is wrong. If they seem to struggle with this, give an additional clue that in all three sentences, the commas are incorrectly used.

Look for the following responses:
Sentence 1 – The comma is used instead of a full stop. There are two quite distinct sentences.
Sentence 2 – The comma is used instead of a full stop. There are three quite distinct sentences.
Sentence 3 – The 'and' at the beginning is not automatically wrong, but it does probably follow on from the list of things about John (brown ...fit...healthy...) in the second sentence, not the comment about Jenny. It pops up as an afterthought.

2 Return to the commas. Ask pupils to tell you when commas are used in sentences. Look for the responses:
- To separate items in a list.
- At the junction between speech and the speaker tag (e.g. he said).
- Between the main clause and subordinate clause where the subordinate clause has been moved to the start or the middle of the sentence.

3 Now ask pupils to suggest, sentence by sentence, ways of correcting the grammar.
Sentence 1 – replace the comma with: a full stop, or a conjunction (joining word) such as 'and' or 'but', or a semi-colon (which can be used to splice together clauses without the use of a joining word.

Sentence 2 – as above. Here, however, you need to scan the overall effect, which may be clumsy. Suggest contracting the sentence into a list to be less cumbersome, e.g. He was brown, fit and healthy, but she looked all weedy and pale in comparison.

Sentence 3 – either add to the end of the list about John or introduce a connective e.g. moreover, what is more.

B6 Commas

> **AIM:** To identify the way commas are used to insert 'asides' and 'extras' into a sentence

YOU WILL NEED:
▶ OHT B6.1
▶ Handout B6.2 enough for one per pupil

1 Look at the first two sentences on OHT B6.1. Ask pupils: What is the difference in meaning between these two sentences? The first tells us that the writer hates boys only if they are idiots. The second tells that us that the writer hates all boys because (s)he considers them all to be idiots. The comma has a significant role

2 Use the second set of sentences to repeat the point.

3 Now invite pupils to make up an example of their own in pairs, and share these.

4 Draw out the idea that commas are used to signal 'asides'. They act rather like brackets, dropping extra information into sentences without disturbing the meaning of the main clause.

5 Reveal the sentences in the lower half of the OHT and cover the upper half. They represent different uses of the comma to carve up sentences. Ask pupils if they can articulate these uses of the comma.

6 Distribute Handout B6.2 which is a reference sheet for pupils.

B7 The complex sentence

> **AIM:** To illustrate the different ways of creating complex sentences for effect

YOU WILL NEED:
▶ OHT B7.1

1 Look at the two simple sentences at the top of OHT B7.1. Ask pupils to think of a handful of different ways to combine them into one sentence.

2 Take ideas and reward ambitious examples.

3   Remind pupils of the ways they can join simple sentences (clauses) together by using a conjunction (joining word) or using a semi-colon (instead of a joining word).

4   Show the possible solution ('While Jenny was on the phone to her gang John was crying on his bed') and ask: Is a comma needed? Look for the response: Yes, after the word 'gang' . The subordinate clause is at the beginning of the sentence, so a comma is needed to mark it off from the main clause. The method used to join the sentences in this case is a conjunction (while). Insert the comma.

5   Ask pupils how they could increase the sense of contrast between John and Jenny. Look for responses such as: adding in something about Jenny laughing or gloating, or dropping in contrasting adjectives such as 'gleeful Jenny' and 'dejected John'.

6   Now reveal the first of the three sentences in the lower section of the OHT. Challenge pupils in twos or threes to combine them into one complex sentence. Tell them that they are free to move the clauses around, and to make small changes which make the new sentence more sophisticated or effective. Allow a minute or so and then take suggestions.

7   Repeat this activity with the other two sentences.

B8 Revision

AIM:	To revise aspects of the complex sentence studied in this section

YOU WILL NEED:
▶ Handout B8.1

1   Distribute Handout B8.1 and administer as a test.

Section C: Clarifying meaning

C1 Ambiguity 1

AIM: To identify the causes of ambiguity

YOU WILL NEED:

▶ OHT C1.1

▶ Handout C1.2, enough for one between two

1 Show OHT C1.1. Pose the question: Why are these sentences funny? Allow the class 1 minute in pairs or threes to come up with a hypothesis.

2 If they struggle with this, give them a clue. Look at the words which have more than one meaning: giant   held   roll   waves   over

3 Take suggestions, rewarding good observations. Look for attempts to explain the meanings of the ambiguous words. For example, the word 'waves' means two things here: as a verb, to wave with your hand, and as a noun, the wave in the sea.

4 Distribute the Handout C1.2 to pairs and ask pupils to study the sentences and explain how ambiguity arises in each one. Allow 5 minutes.

5 Debrief, going through each example orally. Continue this activity in the next starter.

C2 Ambiguity 2

AIM: To identify and resolve ambiguity

YOU WILL NEED:

▶ Handout C1.2 from the last session, enough for one between two

1 Return to handout C1.2 and ask pupils to cut up the sheet into separate sentence strips.

2 Ask pupils to sort the strips into piles depending on how the ambiguity arises. In other words, classify the types of ambiguity.

3 Take feedback. Look for:

- Some sentences are ambiguous because a word or two have more than one meaning, and different grammatical functions, e.g. 'They can fish.': 'can' is used as a noun and a verb.

- Some sentences are ambiguous because the words or phrases are in the wrong order, e.g. 'Computer games for sale by a man going abroad in a plastic box with a joystick.'

- Other sentences are ambiguous because the pronouns are misleading, e.g. 'She told him she had been chosen to run'. Who has been chosen, the person speaking, or the person spoken to?

4   As a minimum, ask pupils to record in their notebooks the three types of ambiguity we have learnt – words with more than one meaning, pronouns misplaced, and phrases or words in the wrong sequence.

5   Ask pupils if they can come up with any jokes that depend on ambiguity, e.g. double meaning.

C3 The problem with pronouns

AIM: To identify and resolve ambiguity in the use of pronouns

YOU WILL NEED:
▶ OHT C3.1

1   Show OHT C3.1 and point out the problem with the first sentence. The ambiguity lies in the fact that we do not know who has been selected, the speaker or the person spoken to.

2   Pose the question: How could we rewrite the sentence so that the meaning is clear?

3   If they struggle with this, point out that they need to give names to the speaker and to the person spoken to.

4   Take suggestions, rewarding good attempts.

5   Work through the other sentences, then ask pupils to spend a couple of minutes considering how they actually resolved the ambiguity, and to formulate advice to others. Look for the response:
- Avoid using pronouns when they are too far from the noun they refer to.
- When in doubt, repeat the noun.
- Check that the noun is named to start with.

C4 Resolving ambiguity by sensible sequencing

AIM: To identify and resolve ambiguities arising from poor sequencing

YOU WILL NEED:
▶ Handout C1.2
▶ Handout C4.1, enough for one between two

1   Refer pupils back to the third sentence on Handout C1.2: 'Computer games for sale by a man going abroad in a plastic box with a joystick.'

2   Pose the question: Why is this advertisement ambiguous? In what ways could it be written to resolve the ambiguity? Allow the class 1 minute in pairs or threes to come up with suggestions.

3   Take sensible suggestions, rewarding good attempts. Point out that the advertisement could be expressed in a clearer way by sensible sequencing where the information about the computer, its box and joystick should be as close as possible. The information about the man going abroad would be best left at the very end.

4   Explain the following principle: Related words should be placed as near to one another as possible so it is clear what they refer to.

5   Distribute Handout C4.1 to pairs and ask them to organise the information in the sentences to remove the ambiguity.

C5 Passives

AIM: To revise the passive voice

YOU WILL NEED:
▶ OHT C5.1

1   Show OHT C5.1. Point out the alphabetical structure and the four-word lines, then ask pupils to complete the next line, e.g. Indigo Jackals Kill Leopards. Take a few ideas then ask them to complete the alphabet.

2   Return to the two sentences on the OHT and ask pupils if they can express the headlines in a different order? If they struggle with this, give them a clue. Turn the words in the first sentence round so that Dangermouse comes at the beginning of the line.

If they still find it hard, ask the pupils to add the word 'was' before the verb and the word 'by' after.

3   Take suggestions, rewarding good attempts. For example:
Dangermouse was crushed by an atom bomb.
Hercules was grasped by Emerald Fountains.

● In the first line, Dangermouse comes first, in the subject position and the word 'was' appears before the verb and the word 'by' after the verb. The atom bomb becomes the agent of the action.

● In the second line, Hercules comes first, in the subject position and the word 'was' appears before the verb and 'by' after the verb. The Emerald Fountain becomes the agent of the action.

These are passive sentences.

5   Now ask pupils to write passive versions of their other lines.

6   Continue this starter in C6.

C6 Hiding the agent

AIM: To understand how the passive voice can be used to conceal the agent

YOU WILL NEED:

▶ OHT C5.1 from last session

▶ OHT C6.1

▶ The alphabet headlines started last session

1 Ask pupils if they can rewrite their first headline in a way that allows them not to mention the atom bomb, e.g.

Dangermouse was crushed.

2 Explain that they have re-expressed the sentence in the passive form, and this allows them to leave out the agent – the person or object that acts. The passive becomes a powerful way for hiding the agent. This can be very useful if you don't want to own up to the responsibility for something!

3 Ask them to go through their headlines and try to hide the agent in each sentence. Take feedback.

4 Show OHT C6.1 and ask them to conduct this activity in reverse by providing agents to go in the sentences. Do this as an oral activity.

5 As a minimum, ask pupils to write in their notebooks one sentence:

- as an active sentence

- as a passive sentence.

For example, Jane read the book. – The book was read by Jane.

C7 Laying the blame

AIM: To show how converting from passive to active identifies the agent

YOU WILL NEED:

▶ OHT C7.1

▶ OHT C7.2

1 Remind pupils how we hid the atom bomb in the sentence:

Dangermouse was crushed by an atom bomb.

when it became

Dangermouse was crushed.

The passive becomes a powerful way for hiding the agent (in this case the atom bomb).

2 Show OHT C7.1. In pairs, ask pupils to invent agents for these sentences.

3 Pose the question: How can these be written without 'was' and 'by' and by placing the agent first in the sentence? Essentially this will convert them into active sentences, e.g. Shearer fouled the goalkeeper.

4 Point out the rule for changing passive to active: The active is written without 'was' and 'by' and by placing the agent first in the sentence.

5 Display OHT C7.2 and point out that the sentences have all been expressed in the passive and the agents hidden. Ask pupils to analyse the effect or implication for the reader. This is, in effect, a mini-exercise in literary criticism. The focus is on the impact.

6 Debrief:

- 'Someone's been injured in the playground' – to avoid saying how it happened or who was responsible. It makes the accident sound like an act of God, and avoids getting anyone in trouble.

- 'The biscuits have all been eaten' – to avoid saying who was responsible.

- 'Mrs Tidyheart noticed that dirt had been trodden into the carpet' – because Mrs Tidyheart didn't know who had done it. It also suggests that she has an accusing attitude, looking for a guilty party.

- 'That's it, thought Jenny. I've been lied to once too often!' – expressed to emphasise her perception of herself as victim. The passive does put the victim at the heart of the sentence.

- 'Oldest building to be demolished' – to avoid saying who took what must be a controversial decision.

- 'Burglar shot in bank raid' – to avoid saying who shot him.

- 'Cars parked in reserved bays will be clamped' – to make it sound threateningly official and anonymous.

- 'Litter louts will be prosecuted' – to make it sound threateningly official and anonymous.

- 'Requests for credit will be refused' – another example of official anonymity but also to spare the person behind the counter from embarrassing refusals.

C8 Actives, passives and agents

AIM: To consolidate and apply the use of actives, passives and agency

YOU WILL NEED:
▶ OHT C8.1

1 Show OHT C8.1. Ask pupils to discuss in pairs whether the sentences are:
- expressed in the active or the passive
- reveal the agent or not
- for what reason?

'Please, sir, the science lab window by the football field has been broken.'
Passive – to avoid owning up!

'I saved the day.'
Active – to take the credit.

'Enemy ship sunk – 100 dead.'
Passive – to avoid the negative implications of 'We killed 100 people'.

'We won the election.'
Active – to claim the credit.

'Please, miss, I was pushed over in the playground.'
Passive – to avoid telling on the person who did it.

'I must go because I am late for an important meeting.'
Active – to emphasise the personal urgency.

'The meeting was delayed.'
Passive – to avoid admitting who delayed it.

'A tax increase has been announced.'
Passive – to avoid admitting that you decided to put up taxes.

2 Pose the question: When is it handy to hide the agent? Suggestions might include:
- When you need to keep the name of a friend secret.
- When you don't want to accept responsibility.
- To avoid accusing or blaming someone.

Section D: Time and motion

D1 Tenses 1

AIM:	To explore the range of tenses in English and how they are formed

YOU WILL NEED:
▶ OHT D1.1

1 Ask pupils to explain what a *tense* is. Look for the response that verbs have tense to indicate when they take place.

2 Now ask pupils how the *past tense* is usually made. Look for the answer -ED.

3 Ask for exceptions, less common ways of making the past tense. Look for examples such as make/made, swim/swam, run/ran, give/gave. Do this briefly as you will return to it later.

4 If spelling is an issue, explore the adding of ED if:
   • The word ends in an E (e.g. love – loved).
   • Words which double a consonant because of the short vowel (e.g. drop - dropped).
   • Words ending in consonant + Y (e.g. cry – cried).
   • Words ending in vowel + Y (e.g. play – played).

5 Now move on to the *future tense*. Show the top half of OHT D1.1 as examples of the future tense. Ask pupils to consider if they can come up with a general rule or rules for making the future tense. Allow only a minute.

6 After one minute, take feedback. Look for the conclusion that the future tense is formed by preceding the main verb with an auxiliary verb (usually will, shall or go). Put crudely, there are only two tenses in English – present and past – but we can express the future by using other verbs to help. These are known as auxiliary verbs. Use the bottom section of OHT D1.1 to illustrate the point.

7 Now return to the present tense. Ask pupils to think of different ways of expressing action in the present tense, e.g. I walk, I am walking, I do walk. These are all subtly different, and the difference is signalled by the auxiliary verb. 'I am walking' implies that it is occurring at the moment of expression, whereas 'I walk' can be used in less immediate contexts, e.g. I walk home every day. 'I do walk' is more emphatic.

8 Return to the past tense and ask for different ways of expressing actions that have occurred in the past.
   E.g.   I walked
                I used to walk

I was walking

I had been walking

I did walk

I have been walking

9 Remind pupils of the variety of expression available in writing. Most pupil writing is dominated by the simple (-ED) past tense. The other forms of the tense can give a reflective feel.

D2 Tenses 2

AIM:	To consolidate pupils' awareness of the different tenses available

YOU WILL NEED:

▶ OHT D2.1

▶ D2.2 cut up into cards, enough for one set between two pupils

1 Remind pupils of the different types of tenses considered in the last starter.

2 Show OHT D2.1 and ask volunteers to come out and pick out verbs with a highlighter and tell you the tense.

I *started* at Midhurst Primary School when I *was* nine. I *had been going* to a very small school in Bridlington but my family *moved*. I *have made* lots of new friends here and *I am learning to swim* which *I enjoy* very much. Next September *I will transfer* to a secondary school in Brighton. *I visited* the school once this term and *I can't believe* how large it is. *I am feeling* a bit nervous about it. When the bell *rang*, all the pupils *began to move* to different rooms for different subjects. *I do hope we won't get lost* in the first few days.

3 Turn off the OHT and ask pupils to sort the verbs from the cards on D2.2, into three piles – past, present and future tenses.

4 Ask pupils to further sort the cards into two sub-piles, one for simple verbs and another for verbs which take an auxiliary verb:

	Present time	**Past time**	**Future time**
Simple Verbs	enjoy is	started was moved visited rang	
Main & Auxiliary Verbs	can't believe am feeling do hope	had been going have made began to move	will transfer won't get lost

D3 Auxiliary verbs

AIM:	To secure an understanding of auxiliary verbs

YOU WILL NEED:

▶ OHT D1.1

1 Use the top half of OHT D1.1 to remind pupils of the meaning of main and auxiliary verbs. Ask them to pick out the auxiliary verbs in one colour and main verbs in another. Alternatively use circling and underlining.

2 Remind them that auxiliary verbs help or add something to the timing of the main verb. You could use as an example the difference between *I went, I have gone* and *I had gone.*

3 Introduce the term 'verb phrase' as a term which covers both main and auxiliary verbs.

4 Pose four questions as a problem-solving quiz to the class and give them a few moments between each response to think about their answer.
   - Does the auxiliary verb generally come before or after the main verb? (before)
   - Give two good reasons for splitting the main verb from the auxiliary verb and putting another word in between them. (To form a negative e.g. I shall not go, or to ask a question e.g. Would you like to drink?)

5 Conclude by reminding pupils that the auxiliary verb is versatile – it brings subtle meanings and can be moved around, including moving it around the main verb.

D4 Verb phrases

AIM:	To recognise verb phrases

YOU WILL NEED:

▶ OHT D4.1

▶ D4.2 cut up into cards, enough sets for one between two or three

1 Remind pupils about the term 'verb phrase'. It includes the main verb and the auxiliary verb.

2 Show OHT D4.1 and ask pupils to consider which words constitute the verb phrase. You can, if you wish, warn them that these are particularly tricky examples. What you are asking is where the verb starts and stops.

3 Take feedback and support answers by warning in advance, for example: 'I'm looking for four words in this first one'.

4 Distribute sets of cut up cards from handout D4.2. Use one set between two pupils. The verbs on the cards include prepositions. The task is to match up all the verbs with all the prepositions. Some verbs can take more than one preposition. One solution is:

put paid + to	hand + out
look forward + to	switch + on
look back + on	turn + off
look up + to	wander + off
swimming + in	make + up
calm + down	care + for
cheer + up	rise + up
vote + for	soldier + on

D5 Lonely verbs

AIM:	To identify verbs that require auxiliaries to work

YOU WILL NEED:

▶ OHT D5.1

1 Explain that there are three particular forms of verb that cannot work on their own but need other verbs to help.

2 Use the top section of OHT D5.1 to explain THE INFINITIVE which is made up of two words: to + stem, e.g. to jump, to sing, to think. It is called the infinitive because it is neither past, present nor future: it is expressed as the state of happening.

3 Use the second section to explain THE –ING PARTICIPLE which is made of the stem + -ing suffix, e.g. talking, walking, breaking, and is used to express actions that are in progress, or continuing.

4 Use the third section of the OHT to explain THE –ED PARTICIPLE which is made of the stem + -ed suffix and used with have or was to show actions that have just finished.

5 Remind pupils that these are often (but not always) lonely verbs and need other verbs to help, and pose the question: In each case, which other verbs do they need? Allow 3 or 4 minutes. Encourage pupils to generate answers by thinking up sentences which include these verbs, to find out which other verbs often accompany them. In essence, this is asking pupils to characterise the stem.

6 Look for the following responses:

The participles often come with a *was* or *have* verb,

e.g.

she *was* talking

he *has* practiced

but you can get other verbs,

e.g.

he *stopped* talking

she *started* practicing.

The infinitive often comes with an introductory action,

e.g.

he *began* to talk

she *stopped* to listen.

D6 Irregular verbs 1

AIM: To recognise patterns in the structure of irregular verbs

YOU WILL NEED:

▶ D6.1 cut up into a set of cards enough for one between two or three pupils

1 Remind pupils that irregular verbs were mentioned when you looked at the past tense. Irregular verbs don't obey the usual rules such as adding S or ED when you make another tense.

2 As a quickfire oral exercise, ask for the past tense of the following verbs and ask how the past has been formed, i.e. what was changed.

Shout	▶ add ED
Smile	▶ add D
Cut	▶ no change at all
Learn	▶ add -t
Spend	▶ change final -d to -t
Find	▶ change middle vowel
Catch	▶ change -atch to -aught ending
Buy	▶ bought
Give	▶ change the middle vowel
Keep	▶ change the long ee sound to short e and add final -t

3 Distribute the cards to pairs or threes and ask them to sort the verbs into piles according to the way the past tense is formed. Allow up to 10 minutes.

4 Take feedback. For each classification, ask the pupils if they can add new words to the list.

5 Point out that in Old English, the past tense was made by changing the middle vowel. The words that have survived from this period tend to be basic everyday high-frequency words.

D7 Irregular verbs 2

AIM:	To identify patterns in irregular past tense verbs

YOU WILL NEED:

▶ Handout D7.1, enough for one per pupil

1 Distribute Handout D7.1 to each pupil. Arrange pupils in groups of four to five. They work as a team but record separately.

2 Allow a few minutes to fill the sheet with as many examples as they can think of. The first one in each section has been done.

3 Go through the answers by identifying the group with the most answers in each section and ask them to read out their list. Invite other teams to add any words not mentioned. Move quickly.

D8 Irregular verbs 3

AIM:	To recognise that one can generalise about irregular verbs – they are unusual but not without pattern

1 Ask pupils in groups to generate three lists of *verbs* ending in IND, ING (not the participle) and INK.

2 After a minute or so, tell them that they should be able to find:

4 INDs

9 INGs

7 INKs

Allow another minute or so before helping them to complete their lists.

3 Now ask them to write next to each verb its past tense and identify patterns.

IND

Wind – wound

Bind – bound

Find – found

Grind – ground

ING

Wring – wrung

Sing – sung

Sling – slung

Cling – clung

Ring – rung

Sting – stung

Spring – sprung

Fling – flung

Bring – brought

INK

Stink – stank

Sink – sank

Drink – drank

Link – linked

Ink – inked

Wink - winked

Think – thought

4   Point out that pupils who are unsure about the correct ending ING or INK could probably work it out by referring to the past tense.

D9 Changing tenses

AIM:	To recognise how changing the tense of the verb impacts on the rest of the sentence

YOU WILL NEED:

▶ OHT 9.1

1   Explain to pupils that today's starter will help to reduce a problem that sometimes occurs in drafting.

2   Show OHT D9.1 and ask pupils – orally – to transform the sentence into the past tense. Look for:

Nowadays I go to the cinema regularly.

>>>

In those days I **went** to the cinema regularly.

I hope it will be a hot day tomorrow.

>>>

I **hoped** it **would be** hot **the next day**.

I feel sick because I have eaten eat too much.

>>>

I **felt** sick because I **had eaten** too much.

I can see some people through the window, but I cannot hear what they are saying.

>>>

I **could see** some people through the window, but I **could not** hear what they **were saying**.

Underline the words on the OHT which are changed in the past tense version.

3 Point out that the first verb changed – but what else and why? Give them a moment to think about this.

4 Take feedback, and establish that not only the verbs, but any other element in the sentence which involves some reference to time or the verb must also be changed.

5 Remind pupils that this re-tensing of the whole sentence is important in revising or redrafting work, or in writing from first hand experience, when there is a tendency to relive the moment and thus slip out of the narrative past into the story-telling 'historical present'.

D10 Prevailing tenses

AIM: To identify the prevailing tense in different kinds of writing

YOU WILL NEED:

▶ OHT D10.1

1 Remind pupils that nearly every piece of writing has a mix of tenses in it, but there will be one tense that is the prevailing tense – the one that is generally used.

2 Give as an example *stories*, which are usually told in the past tense.

3 Put up OHT D10.1 and ask pupils to consider what the prevailing tense is in these types of writing.

4 Debrief

1. Jokes – usually in the historic or story-telling present.
    There's this man, see, and…

2. The method section when you write up a scientific experiment – past.
    We put the magnesium in…

3. The conclusions section of a scientific experiment – present imperative.
    Water increases in volume when…

4. A history essay – past.
     Harold lost the battle...

5. Factual information about the natural world, e.g. volcanoes – present.
     Volcanoes erupt when...

6. A party political manifesto – future.
     We shall introduce...

7. An instruction manual – present.
     Attach the nozzle to the...

8. A tourist brochure – present.
     The resort has three beaches...

9. A match report – past.
     Collins scored the winning goal...

10. The morning news – a mix.
     Today, the Prime Minister will announce...
     Yesterday's floods have left...
     The President arrives at Heathrow...
    The morning news is as likely to look forward to the imminent events of the day as it is to report events that have happened.

Section E: Speech

E1 Ground rules

| AIM: | To revise the function of punctuation marks in speech |

YOU WILL NEED:
▶ OHT E1.1

1 Ask the class to tell you some ways of distinguishing which words are spoken in different written texts. For example:

i) Speech marks in prose

ii) Playscript dialogue

iii) Cartoon bubbles.

2 Reveal OHT E1.1 which illustrates these three methods of representing dialogue. Read No 3 aloud and then cover it. Ask pupils to recall all the punctuation marks used. You can remind them that there were five.

3 As each punctuation mark is mentioned ask pupils where it would be placed in the sentence. Look for the answers:

Speech marks – to enclose the words actually spoken.

Capitals – to mark the start of sentences, as always.

Commas – to mark the change from the spoken part and the rest of the sentence; to separate items in Igor's list of tasks.

Question mark – to conclude questions, as always.

Exclamation mark – to conclude exclamation, as always.

4 Explain that speech marks, inverted commas and quotation marks are synonymous terms.

5 Ask pupils to make a note of the ground rules or conventions in their books. The use of commas will be refined in the next starter.

E2 Commas – where exactly do they go?

| AIM: | To recognise function and placing of commas in speech |

YOU WILL NEED:
▶ OHT E2.1
▶ OHT E2.2
▶ Handout E2.3 enough for one between two

1 Explain that you are going to be looking closely at the exact position of the comma in speech.

2 Show OHT E2.1 and remind pupils that the comma marks the change from the spoken part and the rest of the sentence. Pose the question: Where exactly does it go? They will need to look at all three examples in order to generalise.

3 Take suggestions. Look for the response: Immediately before the speech mark.

4 Show OHT E2.2 , and ask them to find three occasions when a comma is not required.

5 Draw out the rule: You do not need commas if there is a question mark or exclamation mark, or if a new sentence starts after the speaker tag, e.g. he said.

6 Ask pupils what happens if the speaker tag is embedded in the middle of a spoken sentence. Look for the response: Commas always go before the speech marks.

7 Ask: What happens if the speaker tag is embedded in speech but doesn't interrupt a sentence? Look for the response: A comma is only used in a sentence containing the speaker tag.

8 Distribute E2.3 enough for one between two. The speech marks and commas have been deleted in this version. Ask pupils to fill them in applying the rules they have just learnt.

9 Debrief by showing E2.2 again, commenting on the rules.

E3 The speaker tag

AIM: To reflect on the position, function and rules governing the speaker tag

YOU WILL NEED:
▶ OHT E2.2
▶ OHT E3.1

1 Point out that most writers using dialogue will leave the speaker tag (the 'he said' or 'she said' phrase) until after the words have been spoken. Use the first sentence on OHT E2.2 to illustrate this, then remove the OHT.

2 Explain further that one drawback with this is that we don't find out who spoke until after the speech is complete. Pose the question: How then, do we know who is speaking? Allow a pause for answers. Look for the responses:
- from the context
- if there's only two people, you know it must be the other one
- sometimes the speech is distinctive or the views expressed recognisable
- sometimes readers allow their eyes to glance ahead.

3 Ask pupils what alternative options there are to using the speaker tag at the end. Look for the response:

- at the beginning, before the words spoken
- embedded in the speech
- not used at all.

Use OHT E3.1 to prompt and illustrate the points.

4 Ask pupils to spend 2 minutes generalising about where the writer positions the speaker tags in this extract. Look for the response: there's an urgency to give the words spoken, but a need to identify the speaker. Writers tend to leave the speaker's name out unless they need to give it. For example, Clare needs to be identified early on, but there are places when the reader can work out who is speaking without the aid of a speaker tag.

5 Ask pupils to work out the rules governing the speaker tag in the sentence. Ask them to generalise about the use of capital letters and commas. Look for the response:

- 'He said' is always lower case unless it lies at the start of a sentence. In this case it has a capital because it is the first letter of a new sentence.
- Commas are placed between speaker tag and speech unless there is a question mark or exclamation mark.

E4 Paragraphing dialogue

AIM:	To identify the conventions governing paragraph breaks in dialogue

YOU WILL NEED:

▶ OHT E3.1

▶ A copy of a current reading book each

1 Return to OHT E3.1 and ask pupils now to look at paragraphing. Pose the question: What is the rule about paragraphs and dialogue? Most pupils have been told that they must start a new line when someone new starts to speak. This isn't strictly true. If you get this response, point them to the opening 'Julie agreed'. Look for the response: Only one person may speak per paragraph.

2 Remind pupils that we start a new paragraph when there is a shift in topic, time or perspective. Inevitably a new speaker creates this shift and so a new paragraph starts. But sometimes the shift happens before the speaker starts. In this case, the focus moved to Julie just before she started to speak.

3 The paragraphing of dialogue is also a help to the reader. It signposts a shift of speaker and allows the writer to give the speech without necessarily having to identify the speaker. Although paragraph indentations are dying out in printed text, most writers have retained indentation for speech punctuation.

4   Ask pupils to look now in their current reading books for a page or so of dialogue and identify how the writer uses paragraphs in dialogue. Allow a minute or so.

5   Take feedback. Draw out the way paragraphs are used for all the usual purposes even in dialogue. In particular:

- Shift in time, topic or perspective.
- Change of speaker.
- For breaking up very long speech contributions (noting that speech marks are left open at the end of paragraphs as a reminder that speech continues).
- For chunks of narrative with or without speech in them.

E5 Dialogue

AIM:	To recognise different styles and patterns in dialogue among famous writers

YOU WILL NEED:

▶ Copies of several novels by different writers to share between groups

▶ Recommended writers include a short story anthology; a diverse mix of older texts such as Austen or Dickens; Alan Garner; teenage pulp fiction featuring large 'casts' and therefore much dialogue

1   Put pupils into groups of four and provide them with 6-8 books for browsing.

2   Ask them to look for pages of dialogue in order to examine the writer's favoured way of presenting dialogue. Ask them to look for how the writer:

- identifies speakers
- positions the speaker tag ('he said' phrase)
- paragraphs the shifts between narrative and dialogue.

3   If you are referring to a class novel, you might wish to pre-select a page to use, and draw out the characteristics of your current writer.

4   Take feedback, identifying writers who like spare dialogue and leave the reader to do much of the work in identifying the speaker (Alan Garner is one of these). You will also find that teenage texts feature much shorter speeches, but because they have a large 'casts', they tend to identify speakers more consistently.

E6 Alternatives to 'exclaimed'

AIM: To widen the range of verbs used in dialogue

YOU WILL NEED:

▶ OHT E6.1

1 Show the first section only of OHT E6.1 and ask pupils to suggest a phrase to follow, such as 'he said' e.g. exclaimed, shouted, yelled.

2 Point out the way that the content and exclamation mark tells the reader how the words are spoken – with surprise, abruptness, often with volume.

3 Put pupils into groups and ask them to write the alphabet down the margin of a shared sheet. The task is to find a synonym for *exclaimed* to go against as many letters as possible. Allow 3 minutes.

4 Take feedback. Praise those who have collected a lot of words. Probe the slight differences of meaning, e.g. shrieked & shouted; bellowed & blared.

Announced
Bellowed, blared, blurted, barked, bawled, bayed, boomed
Cried, called, commanded, complained, cheered, clamoured, chanted
Declared
Exclaimed, exploded
F
G
Howled
Insisted
J
K
L
M
N
Ordered
Protested
Q
Roared, ranted
Shrieked, shouted, screamed, squealed, snapped, screeched
Thundered
Urged
V
Wailed
X
Yelled, yelped
Z

4 Display the collected results on a wall poster and make A4 copies for pupils to keep as a reference for writing.

E7 Alternatives to 'asked'

AIM:	To widen the range of verbs used in dialogue

1 Remind pupils of the alphabet constructed in the last starter for synonyms of 'exclaimed', and invite them to repeat this activity for words to use in dialogue when a question has been asked.

2 Allow a few minutes then take feedback.

Answered, asked, appealed, advised
Begged, beseeched
Challenged, canvassed
Demanded
Enquired, entreated
F
Grilled
H
Implored, interrogated
J
K
L
M
N
O
Probed, pleaded, pried
Queried, questioned, quizzed
Requested
Sought
T
U
V
Wheedled, wondered
X
Y
Z

3 Display the collected results on a wall poster and make A4 copies for pupils to keep as a reference for writing.

E8 Alternatives to 'said'

AIM:	To widen the range of verbs used in dialogue

1 Remind pupils of the alphabets constructed in the last two starters for synonyms of 'exclaimed' and 'asked', and invite them to repeat this activity in groups for words to use in dialogue instead of 'said'. This is a broad category, but excludes the words given in previous starters.

2 Allow a few minutes then take feedback.

Agreed, affirmed, argued, asserted, answered, acknowledged, alleged, admitted, averred

B

Commented, croaked, continued, chirped, confided, countered

Drawled, droned

Explained, echoed

Fretted

Gabbled, gushed, groaned

Hissed

Intoned, interjected, informed, insisted

Joked

K

Laughed

Murmured, muttered, maintained, mumbled

N

Observed, offered

Prattled, proposed, pronounced, proclaimed

Quipped

Replied, remarked, retorted, responded, rambled, returned, rejoined, rebutted

Stated, said, sobbed, spluttered, summarised, sniggered, suggested

Teased

Uttered

Vowed

Whispered, warned, whimpered

X

Yabbered

Z

3 Ask pupils to divide their words (e.g. by underlining and circling) between those which describe the function (e.g. replied, continued) and those which describe the sound of the speech (e.g. whispered, croaked).

4 Show pupils how one might convey both sound and function by converting the sounds into adverbs, e.g. 'answered chirpily'. Ask them to suggest further combinations.

5 Display the collected results on a wall poster and make A4 copies for pupils to keep as a reference for writing.

Section F: Paragraphs

F1 Cues to start a new paragraph 1

AIM: To recognise cues to start a new paragraph

YOU WILL NEED:

▶ OHT F1.1

▶ F1.2 as an OHT and Handouts, enough for one between two

1 Show OHT F1.1, and read the extract aloud.

2 Pose the question: There are seven paragraphs in this extract. I want you to explain why each one starts where it does. In other words, how did the writer know he needed to start a new paragraph?
Allow the class to work in pairs for a few minutes to come up with reasons for each new paragraph.

3 Take suggestions, rewarding good observations. Look for the following responses:

- When there is a change in topic/subject.
- When there is a shift in time.
- When there is a change in viewpoint.
- When someone new starts to speak.

4 Distribute the Handout F1.2 to pairs and ask them to:
a) identify where paragraphs should be inserted
b) give the reasons why each one starts where it does.
Allow 3-4 minutes.

5 Take answers. Mark on your copy of the OHT where the paragraphs should begin so pupils can check their decisions:
a) Claire Guthrie...   d) Ben wasn't...
b) Instead of...   e) Claire's eyes...
c) 'Claire,' said Di...   f) 'Sorry,' she said...

6 Ask pupils to record reasons for using new paragraphs in their books.

F2 Cues to start a new paragraph 2

AIM: To recognise cues to start a new paragraph

YOU WILL NEED:

▶ OHT F2.1

▶ F2.2 as an OHT and a Handout for each pupil

1 Read aloud (but do not show) the extract on OHT F2.1. Make sure the paragraph breaks are conveyed in your shifts of tone and in the pauses. The first time you read it, they just need to listen.

2 On your second reading, ask pupils to put up a hand when they think you have moved into a new paragraph. Stop almost immediately and ask why, e.g. change of time, viewpoint, etc.

3 Show pupils the extract on the OHT to consolidate their understanding.

4 Distribute Handout F2.2 and ask pupils, in small groups, to identify where the five paragraphs start and why.

5 Take responses using an OHT of F2.2, drawing out the reasons for the shift of paragraph. Paragraphs start at:

- It was the enemy...
- Alex had felt...
- Who had sent him?
- Alex took the quad...
- He should have been dead...

6 Next, ask the pairs to rehearse a dramatic reading of the passage, emphasising the paragraph changes to their audience. Your aim here is to draw attention to the oral cues which signal a shift of topic, viewpoint or time. Pupils could emphasise the change in viewpoint by having someone else read that paragraph.

7 Watch some performances, rewarding effective ways of conveying paragraph changes.

F3 Paragraph Structure 1

AIM: To identify paragraphs structured by chronology, causation and order of importance

YOU WILL NEED:

▶ OHT F3.1

1 Use OHT F3.1 to remind pupils about topic sentences at the start of paragraphs.

2 Then ask pupils to look at the rest of paragraph A and ask how the writer must have determined the order of sentences within it. Look for the answer: by order of event or chronology. Point to the tell-tale connectives. Find one and ask pupils to spot the others: *First... Then... After that...*

3 Do the same with paragraph B and look for the answer: by cause and effect. Point to the tell-tale vocabulary of logical links. Find one and ask

pupils to spot the others: *the result of… causing… are caused when… is created by… and thus…*

4 Do the same with paragraph C and look for the answer: by order of importance or hierarchy. Point to tell-tale links. Find one and ask pupils to spot the others: *The first and most important reason is… it also allows… even if… then at least… in future…*

5 Complete this activity in the next starter.

F4 Paragraph structure 2

AIM:	To identify paragraphs structured by chronology, causation and order of importance

YOU WILL NEED:

▶ F4.1 cut up into separate cards, enough sets for one between two or three

1 Remind pupils of the three types of paragraphs discussed in the last starter: chronology, importance and cause & effect.

2 Distribute the sets of cards on F4.1 to pairs or threes and allow a few minutes for them to determine the type of organisation in each paragraph and to highlight the giveaway vocabulary. To differentiate, pupils could be given selected paragraphs only.

3 Take feedback, identifying key features of the paragraph which help to identify which structure had been used. Discuss any differences in opinion.

F5 Paragraph structure 3

AIM:	To identify paragraphs structured around a point, an example and a conclusion

YOU WILL NEED:

▶ F5.1 cut into paragraph cards, enough for one between three

1 Set pupils an investigation: Working in groups of four, they have 5 minutes to determine how the paragraphs they have been given have been structured. To assist them further, you may wish to explain that each paragraph has three different sections or parts. (This information could be used to differentiate the activity at the start, or mentioned if any groups need additional support after a few minutes.)

2 Take suggestions from groups and record these. When recording, write synonyms together so the pupils can see the similarity in their answers. You may collect:

- Point, assertion, main idea, statement.
- Example, evidence, proof, illustration.
- Conclusion, summary, implications.

3 As a class, determine the structure: point, example(s), conclusion.

4 Invite the class to compose, orally, paragraphs which use the same structure, on topics such as Recent Music, Really Bad TV Programmes or How to Survive Lunchtime.

5 Listen to some of the paragraphs. The rest of the class identify each of the sections of each paragraph.

F6 Paragraph structure 4

AIM: To consider the best way to organise paragraphs containing diverse points of equal weight

YOU WILL NEED:

▶ OHT F6.1, but cut the OHT into strips so that the points can be rearranged

1 Remind pupils that you have been looking at paragraph structure and found that most paragraphs have a guiding principle to help organise ideas in them, e.g. sequenced in time or by order of importance. Explain the trickiness of writing a paragraph in which the points are related by content but have no obvious order.

2 Display the strips of OHT 6.1 to illustrate the point. Ask pupils to suggest a possible sequence for this disparate group of points. Start by asking if they can see any items that might go together or follow on from another. Rearrange the points on the projector as you go.

3 Once the points are assembled, ask pupils to word a topic sentence to open with, and a closing sentence to conclude on.

4 Now ask them how they might link the points together with connecting words and phrases. Whatever order they have come up with, the key question is the same: how to stop it sounding fragmented like a list. Focus on the possible connecting words.

5 Draw out:

- The use of the opening and closing sentence to bring some coherence.
- That some points cluster together, but others don't.
- The importance of links between points.

F7 Paragraph diagrams 1

AIM: To conceptualise the structure of paragraphs in diagrammatic form

YOU WILL NEED

▶ F5.1 reproduced as a handout for each pupil

▶ OHT F7.1

▶ OHT F7.2

1 Some pupils find it easier to think of paragraph structure in visual form. Put up OHT F7.1 and ask pupils to identify which of the images represents the structure of a paragraph organised by:

> Point – three examples – conclusion
>
> Chronology (order of event)
>
> Cause and effect.

2 When they offer an answer, ask them how they worked it out, e.g.

- the point leads to the conclusion via three equal examples
- chronology is a time sequence represented here as a spatial sequence
- cause and effect happen in time but also bring about change represented here by the change of shape in the boxes.

3 Refer pupils to Handout F5.1 and ask them to find the two paragraphs in it that correspond to the diagram at the top of the page (C and F). Use the top half of OHT F7.2 to exemplify the right answer for C.

4 Now ask pupils to draw a blank of the diagram and fill it in to represent the content of paragraph F. Use the bottom half of F7.2 to debrief if you wish.

F8 Paragraph diagrams 2

AIM: To conceptualise the structure of paragraphs in diagrammatic form

YOU WILL NEED:

▶ F4.1 as a handout or on cards

▶ Six blank A3 sheets per group

1 To consolidate the work done so far, put pupils in groups to produce giant diagrams of the paragraphs on F4.1 on each of the blank sheets. Tell them that they should not feel bound to stick with the types of diagram offered in the last starter but may develop their own.

2 To start them off, do the first paragraph with them. You may well come up with a star chart:

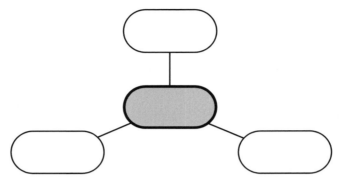

3 Now work through the paragraphs, stopping after two minutes for each one and asking pupils to hold up their sheets so the rest of the class can see. Reward clear successful ideas.

4 If you find this a useful starter, you can extend it quite easily. Encourage creativity. For example, they could use a hamburger to represent the 'point – evidence – conclusion' structure or a bowl of fruit to represent a cluster of like-points. Encourage pupils to think of their own ideas to represent the structure of their paragraphs. Groups can display their work and can be rewarded for good conceptual outlines.

F9 Paragraph diagrams 3

AIM: To select appropriate paragraph structures for given information

YOU WILL NEED:

▶ Handout F9.1 enough for one between two

1 Distribute Handout F9.1 to pairs and explain to pupils the task of designing paragraph shapes into which this information can be poured. Allow 7 minutes, one for each paragraph. Ask them to sketch quick diagrams for each paragraph.

2 Take feedback. Discuss suggestions as a class and reward effective ideas.

3 Continue with this activity in the next starter.

F10 Paragraph composition 1

AIM: To compose a well-shaped and coherent paragraph

YOU WILL NEED:

▶ Handout F9.1 enough for one between two
▶ The related diagrams from the last starter

1   Refer back to the work done in the last starter.

2   Remind pupils of the meaning of the word *connective* – a word or phrase that can be used to connect ideas.

3   Ask pupils what connectives may be used between the different points in their diagram for paragraph B, e.g.

  - On one hand…
  - Equally...
  - Another issue is…

4   Now ask them to write up their paragraphs. Afterwards, share and compare examples, rewarding well-linked and coherent writing.

5   If you have more time, or wish to spend further starters on this, move on to D, E and F on Handout F10.1.

F11 Paragraph composition 2

AIM:	To compose a well-shaped and coherent paragraph

YOU WILL NEED:

▶   Handout F11.1

1   Explain to pupils that previously they have structured paragraphs using fairly detailed bulleted points. For this task, they will need to provide their own connectives and where necessary rearrange the order of some of the ideas.

2   Tackle one paragraph at a time so that you can stop to share and compare efforts, drawing out successful strategies. Remind pupils to determine the structure of each paragraph graphically before they write the paragraph. As in the previous starter, they need to insert appropriate connectives and additional phrases to complete sentences and create meaningful paragraphs.

3   Listen to some examples, rewarding effective paragraph construction.

F12 Paragraph organisation

AIM:	To organise the material for several paragraphs

YOU WILL NEED:

▶   F12.1 as an OHT or handout

1   Explain to pupils that previously they have structured paragraphs using bulleted points that have already been divided into paragraphs for them.

For this task, they need to accurately structure a set of paragraphs from a whole cluster of key ideas. They will also need to rearrange the order of some of the ideas and possibly omit a few points if they do not logically fit anywhere.

2   Show OHT F12.1. Select four pupils and give each one a highlighter pen of different colours. Allocate each pupil a topic which will eventually become a paragraph:

- Appearance
- Behaviour
- Hunting
- Females

Now work through the list and ask the class to place each statement under a heading so that the selected pupils highlight each point in the correct colour. Some will be debatable, especially around Females and Hunting. Mark them in both colours. In fact, these are very useful statements as they offer flexibility later because they will slot into different places. This is a point you should make to the pupils.

3   Take the statements highlighted for Hunting.

- Ask the pupils to identify overlap and decide which ones to delete as redundant or not adding much.
- Then ask pupils to identify points which seem to go together or follow each other.
- Then ask pupils in what order the points should go and how they might be linked.
- Finally ask pupils to write up the hunting paragraph.

4   Share and compare efforts, rewarding coherent paragraphs.

5   You could use further starters to develop the other paragraphs in the same way.

(F13) Paragraph links and signposts 1

AIM:	To recognise the use of pronouns as a cohesion device

YOU WILL NEED:

▶ OHT F13.1

1   Read aloud the top half of OHT F13.1. It is clumsy because of the repetition of the nouns and noun phrases. Ask pupils to identify ways in which it could be improved. Annotate the OHT as they give their suggestions. You should end up with a paragraph similar to:

> The man went to take his dog for a walk. He called Toto, his dog, and showed him his lead. As they were leaving the house, his daughter explained that she would like to join them for a walk to the florist. She wanted to buy a bouquet of flowers for her aunt, who was recovering from an operation and she planned to visit her later in the evening.

2 Explain that one of the ways in which paragraphs are 'glued together' is through the use of pronouns. These help us to make links between different ideas without the fuss of pointless repetition. Pronouns refer back to subjects that have already been introduced and those that will follow.

3 Pose the question: Not all nouns are converted into pronouns. How does a writer decide when it's okay to use a pronoun and when to stick with the noun? Look for the responses:

- The first mention should be the noun.
- The context should make it easy for the reader to work out who (or what) the pronoun refers to.

4 Show the bottom half of the OHT and allow pupils time, in groups, to rewrite it. Once they have done this, ask them to look again to see if there are any improvements in expression they could suggest to make the paragraph more fluent and natural. Share and compare results. The use of WH words (such as who, where and which) is a common device for shortening and clarifying sentences.

F14 Paragraph links and signposts 2

AIM:	To recognise the use of connectives as a cohesion device

YOU WILL NEED:

▶ OHT F14.1 or produced as a large poster for the wall

▶ OHT F14.2

1 Display F14.1 and ask pupils to decide what kind of job each group of words performs and when one might use them:

1 = to extend an idea

2 = to sequence actions

3 = to compare ideas

4 = to contrast ideas

5 = to qualify ideas

6 = to exemplify

7 = to link cause and effect

8 = to conclude

If the pupils have difficulty, you could offer a random answer and ask them to say which group of words it fits.

2 Show OHT F14.2 and invite pupils to combine the related sentences, orally, using suitable connectives. Explain that it may be necessary to omit some of the words of the original paragraph when the link words are inserted.

F15 Paragraph links and signposts 3

AIM: To recognise the use of connectives in binding a paragraph

YOU WILL NEED

▶ OHT F15.1

▶ Handout F15.2

1 Show OHT F15.1 and explain that the task is similar to that in the last starter, but that on this occasion, as well as joining ideas, the sentences have to be trimmed and tightened so that they read well. Make amendments on the OHT. Ask pupils for connectives to link the sentences together, but as you go, read aloud the results and ask for ways of improving the expression. Most often this will involve deleting words and integrating sentences together.

2 Distribute Handout F15.2 and invite the pupils to link and tighten the sentences by writing amendments straight onto the sheet.

3 Share and compare answers, rewarding economical and fluent expression.

F16 Key sentences

AIM: To alert pupils to the significance and positioning of the key sentence in a paragraph

YOU WILL NEED:

▶ F16.1 as an OHT and handout

1 Explain that most paragraphs contain a sentence which is 'key' in understanding it. The most obvious one is that which they have learnt about before – an opening sentence which summarises the topic of the paragraph ('topic sentence'). But not all key sentences come at the beginning and not all of them do a 'summarising' job.

2 Show OHT F16.1 and distribute copies among pairs. Ask pupils to read through and identify the sentence they consider to be the key or main sentence in each paragraph.

3 Debrief making these points as you go:
- The first paragraph – sentence 1
- The second paragraph – sentence 1 introduces the topic (prides) but the final sentence rounds up all the information offered and draws it together in a summarising conclusion.
- The third paragraph – this paragraph pursues two closely-linked themes (the lioness and the hunt), and there is no overarching sentence. Instead, the writer has used sentences 1 and 2 to introduce the topics.

- The fourth paragraph – clearly sentence 1, but ask pupils why it is. This is the place to draw out the significance of generalisations over specifics.
- The fifth paragraph has no obvious key sentence though the paragraph is themed around an observation of the lions. There is a key word (lions) at the start, however. Readers are left to make connections for themselves. It is not an absolute rule that paragraphs contain a key sentence.

F17 Grabbing the reader's attention in the first line

> **AIM**: To identify the tactics used by writers to grab attention in the first line of narrative

YOU WILL NEED:

▶ Handout F17.1

1 Distribute copies of Handout F17.1. Explain that this is a selection of opening lines. Set them a 5-minute investigation for groups: What tactics can a writer use to grab attention in the first sentence?

2 Collate suggestions on the board, for example:
- A problem or dilemma is introduced.
- Something unusual has happened.
- There is an element of challenge – like a dare.
- The author says something that the reader can relate to.
- The author says something unexpected or unconventional.
- There is unusual or interesting imagery.
- The reader is stimulated to want to know more.

3 Ask pupils to copy these into their books, or display the list on a poster.

4 Pupils write their own opening sentences which grab the reader's attention in the first line. Ask for volunteers to offer their sentences. Reward genuinely interesting ideas.

F18 Punchline conclusions 1

> **AIM**: To alert pupils to the tactic of punchline conclusions

YOU WILL NEED:

▶ OHT F18.1

1 Use OHT F18.1 to alert pupils to the use of one-line paragraphs as concluding punchlines. Draw attention to the way the final line in the first extract signals a sense of arrival, completion and conclusion.

2 Ask pupils why the last line in the second paragraph has been separated off. Look for the response: it signals a sudden shock.

3 If you are currently reading a novel or story with the class, refer them to similar examples in the text.

F19 Punchline conclusions 2

AIM:	To alert pupils to the tactic of punchline conclusions

YOU WILL NEED:
▶ Handout F19.1

1 Distribute Handout F19.1 and ask pupils in groups to identify how the punchline delivers its punch in each case. Allow 5 minutes.

2 Take feedback and look for the following points:
- *Burning up* – signals shared purpose and harmony: a common theme at the end of narrative. It is a reassuring ending because something positive is going to happen.
- *Stormbreaker* – the words 'disappeared' and 'dying light' prepare the reader for the end of the story. The reader experiences the end of the story in much the same was as Alex witnesses the departure of the helicopter: it recedes away.
- *Throwaways* – a sour moment suddenly comes right with a hint of romance. Harmony is restored.
- *Dear Nobody* – the writer moves out of narrative action into simile, pulling away from the events to comment on the bigger picture.

3 Make the obvious point that the single-line paragraph is a visual signal to the reader, who sees it and expects a strong, self-explanatory statement.

4 Allow 2 or 3 minutes for groups to brainstorm a number of tactics used by writers to give a punchy conclusion.

5 Collate the criteria on the board. Look for the following suggestions, as well as any other appropriate ideas the pupils may suggest:
- A short summative sentence.
- A sense of completion or finality.
- An acceptance of the past.
- Order being restored.
- A sense of harmony.
- Hope for the future.
- Imagery or symbolism.

Section G: The shape of writing

G1 Signposts

AIM:	To alert pupils to ways of directing the reader's attention through a text

YOU WILL NEED:

▶ OHT G1.1

1 Show OHT G1.1 and explain that writers offer signposts to readers to guide them through paragraphs using connecting phrases which lead attention from one idea to the next. They could be described as hooks.

2 Take a highlighter pen and ask pupils to read through with you, picking out the opening words of each sentence to see if it signals to the reader what is coming. You should pick out:

- connectives (italicised below)
- opening phrases which help to establish quickly the topic of the sentence (underlined below).

3 Once they have got the idea, ask them to work on this in groups on the handout.

<u>Circuses are</u> popular for a variety of reasons. <u>They are</u> an excellent form of entertainment, appealing to the whole family. *For example*, they have magicians, to enchant the audience; clowns, for laughter, tricks and fun; animals to perform tricks; and trapeze artists, who impress with their gymnastic skill.

Looking beyond the glamour of the performance, however, some people are critical of what they offer. <u>The humour of the clowns</u> can be cruel, and the treatment of animals humiliating.

Furthermore, opponents of circuses have real concerns about the living conditions and treatment of the animals. <u>Many circus animals are caged</u> in confined spaces that are totally unnatural environments for them. They were not created to perform tricks in order to earn rewards or treats, and they are certainly not intended to perform in front of large noisy audiences. <u>It is these aspects of the circus</u> that people who defend the rights of animals find difficult to support.

On the other hand, supporters commend the close bonds that develop between animals and their trainers. *Moreover*, they claim that circuses help to conserve endangered species.

To sum up, circuses have their critics, but despite this large numbers of people enjoy attending circus performances.

4 As an extension, look for hooks and signposts within sentences. Words like 'furthermore' and the use of pronouns are worthy of mention. Cohesion is also secured by repeating structures, for example in the second sentence.

G2 Layout

AIM:	To alert pupils to the significance of lay-out in conveying meaning

YOU WILL NEED:
- ▶ OHT G2.1
- ▶ OHT G2.2
- ▶ A blank OHT

1 Show OHTs G2.1 and G2.2 and explain that three different types of text have been converted into a symbols font. Pose the question: Can you work out the nature of the original text?

2 Take answers:
- Story
- Instructions
- Letter
- Poster

3 The key question is: How did you know? What were the tell-tale clues? This should lead you to a discussion of lay-out features including:
- Size of font, e.g. banner headlines on poster.
- Position of text, e.g. centring in poster or flushing left in prose.
- Line breaks, e.g. listing instruction but run-on lines in prose.
- Conventional layouts as in letter.

4 Ask pupils: If we had seen the letter font, would that have added any further presentation features? As a hint, you could refer them to the font option on a computer. This should lead them to consider the use of italics, font style, boldface and underlining.

5 Now ask pupils to sketch out in rough and using a wiggly line for lines of print, the layout for a range of text types, one per group. For example:

a recipe

a poem

a playscript

a memo

a school report

a write up of a science experiment.

6 Distribute a blank OHT to each group to do a neat copy, then ask them to display their efforts to the rest of the class. The other groups guess what it is. This could be organised as a quiz, with answers last. Draw out the clues in the layout.

7 Finish off by saying that most untidy work can be improved by the use of space and careful layout. The use of space is one of the quickest ways of improving the appearance of untidy handwriting.

G3 Organising argument 1

AIM: To consider the most effective way of organising points in an argument

YOU WILL NEED

▶ OHT G3.1 cut up as transparency cards

1 Explain to pupils the meaning of the word 'argument' in this context: the consideration of two opposing points of view.

2 Show OHT G3.1 cut as separate transparent cards arranged randomly on the projector. Ask pupils to suggest two ways in which these points could be sensibly organised.

3 Look for:
- Introducing the topic, then outlining the arguments from one point of view, followed by the arguments from the other point of view, and then reaching a conclusion. Show this arrangement on the OHT by placing the cards in a vertical line.
- Introducing the topic, then dealing with each point and opposing point in turn until all the main arguments have been discussed, and then reaching a conclusion. Show this by arranging the opposing points in pairs.

4 Discuss the benefits and limitations of each arrangement. Whilst the first solution may be easy, the second solution allows for more comparison, and the capacity to respond to or qualify points.

5 Ask pupils what kind of connectives might be used as they shift from point to point. Focus on specific joins – this isn't a general question, e.g.
on one hand...
on the other hand...
critics argue that...

6 Continue this topic in the next starter.

G4 Organising argument 2

AIM: To consider the most effective way of organising points in an argument

YOU WILL NEED:

▶ OHT G4.1 (plus handouts for one between each group of four to six)

1 Recapitaluate the benefits of organising opposing points in pairs or like groups.

2 Distribute Handout G4.1 and show it on the OHT also. Explain that the points for and against have been alternated on the left hand side, leaving the right hand column free for evidence, example or illustration.

3 Work on a particular example such as 'School uniform should be abolished', taking quick oral suggestions and filling in the boxes with supporting points. Comment as you go on the sense of grouping points together if they are connected or if they respond to a previous point.

4 Ask pupils to work on the sheet in groups, focusing on different topics such as:
- Getting the vote at age 11.
- Paying over-11s a standard rate of pocket money.
- Jailing parents for under-age smoking.
- Government funding for a computer for every home.

A scribe will write up and display the completed OHT.

5 Share and compare plans, drawing out any issues about the grouping and ordering of points.

G5 Organising information

AIM: To consider the most effective way of organising points in informative writing

YOU WILL NEED:

▶ Handout G5.1 cut into strips for sequencing, one set per pair of pupils

1 Explain the problem about organising information: it does not come in order of time, so a different way of organising it must be found – perhaps by order of importance, interest, age, alphabetical order, etc.

2 Give pupils the sequencing strips about Brazil made up from Handout G5.1 (2 pages). Working in pairs, their task is to sequence the text in a suitable order for a single entry in a children's encyclopaedia.

3 After a few minutes, take feedback from the class. The precise order of paragraphs is not as important as using a sensible method of grouping and sequencing points. Look for the following:

- The opening statement which explains what the text includes.
- The key facts at the beginning of the information.
- The geographical features correctly identified and sequenced (a, b, and c points).
- The extra information about deforestation following the bullet points which identify the environmental problems.
- The hierarchy of size and presentation in the sub-headings.
- Length can be an indicator or sequence: the more important points get more space.
- Using connectives and context cues to sequence the paragraphs about recreation.
- The glossary at the end.

4 Ask pupils to suggest what else may be included in a non-chronological information text. Look for the following:

- diagrams or illustrations
- graphs or tables
- formal subject specific terminology (e.g. classification, habitat)
- a table of contents, list of references, etc.

G6 Comparison and contrast 1

AIM:	To consider the most effective way of organising comparisons and contrasts

YOU WILL NEED:

▶ OHT G6.1 cut up into transparent cards
▶ OHT G6.2 cut up into transparent cards

1 Ask pupils what they think the difference may be between comparing and contrasting. Look for the response that one looks for likeness and the other for differences.

2 Point out that at this level, one rarely makes pure comparisons or contrast, but a mix of both, drawing out similarities and differences. It is also true that the process is pretty similar: setting two things side by side and looking across.

3 Put up the transparent cards made from OHT G6.1 and arrange them randomly on the screen. Ask pupils to suggest how they might arrange these points if they were to write an essay comparing and contrasting two items. They may well suggest a format like that used for argument in G3 –

alternating points of comparison with points of contrast, but you need to point out some of the difficulties of switching tack, in this case: the reader loses a sense of direction because each 'card' already has within it two texts which are compared, and the swapping between texts is too cluttered and frantic. Encourage them to the conclusion that one needs to work through the comparisons first and then the contrasts.

4 Next put up the transparent cards made from OHT G6.2 and arrange them randomly on the screen. Ask pupils to help you to sort them into three columns of words that can be useful to compare, contrast or give an overview.

G7 Comparison and contrast 2

AIM:	To consider the most effective way of organising comparisons and contrasts

YOU WILL NEED:

▶ OHT G7.1 as an OHT and as handouts, enough for one between each group of four

1 Show OHT G7.1 and take a simple topic such as Y7 and Y9 pupils. Go through the headings on OHT and pencil in one or two word prompts, some of which you can provide and some of which pupils may provide. Zoom through this at high speed, and make a virtue of pace. It is essential that you take no more than 4 minutes to do this. Speed makes planning attractive: more pupils will do it if they know it is quick and still helps.

Introducing the two items to be compared:
   Y7/Y9 pupils

An obvious similarity:
   same school, same teachers, etc

Another obvious similarity:
   appearance – school uniform

A less obvious similarity:
   similar social background – live in locality

An obvious difference:
   tastes and interests

Another obvious difference:
   Y7 new, Y9 approaching end KS3/SATs etc

A less obvious difference:
   Y7 genders split – Y9 mix more

Overview:
Similarities stronger than differences.

Conclusion:
A lot to look forward to – each age is special.

2 Distribute a blank sheet to groups of four or five and give them 4 minutes to brainstorm different topics in the same way, e.g.

History & Geography.

The original Star Wars or the latest version.

Two popular computer games.

Rival bands.

Two popular theme parks.

Two F1 teams.

Two football clubs.

3 Take a team that has finished and ask them to dash through their plan with the class. Take another couple of volunteers if you have time.

4 Remind the class how valuable it is to spend a minute on a simple plan in examination conditions and before writing anything substantial.

Section H: Pace and punch

H1 Short breathless sentences

AIM: To illustrate the effect of writing short sentences

YOU WILL NEED:
▶ OHT H1.1

1 Show the top section of OHT H1.1 and point out that all these sentences have something in common: they are trying to communicate a moment of panic, danger or drama. Allow about 30 seconds for pairs to discuss what they notice about the sentence construction – not what it says but how it is written.

2 Take feedback. Look for the responses which say that the sentences are all:
   • short
   • heavily punctuated
   • sometimes alliterated.

3 Invite the class to say the sentences aloud and notice what effect this has on them when they say it. Look for the answer: it recreates a breathless delivery.

4 Show the middle section of the OHT and challenge the class to re-express it in short breathless sentences. Do this orally, rewarding good efforts.

5 Show the lower section of the OHT and repeat the activity individually.

6 Share and compare answers, rewarding good efforts.

H2 Tension

AIM: To consider the use of short sentences to communicate tension

YOU WILL NEED:
▶ OHT H2.1

1 Read aloud the top section of OHT H2.1 and point out that it describes a moment of high drama. Remind pupils that writers have a number of techniques for inducing feelings of tension and excitement in readers, and one of these techniques is the use of sentence length and punctuation. Ask pupils to discuss in twos or threes how the writer has used length and punctuation to increase the tension. Allow 2 minutes.

2 Take feedback. Pupils should notice that the sentences are short and rather choppy. In fact, they get shorter to increase the tension.

3 Ask pupils to take another minute of discussion to reflect on why short choppy sentences communicate a sense of tension or panic.

4 Take feedback. Look for the response that it simulates the physical sensation of panic through breathlessness and hopping from one perception to the next very rapidly.

5 Show the middle section of OHT H2.1 and ask pupils to look for a similar effect in the dialogue. Look for the responses:
  - Short utterances, only one or two words long.
  - Rapidly changing punctuation – questions, exclamations, trailing ends, etc.
  - Later utterances not attributed to speakers, thus shortening the dialogue line.
  - Lack of connectives – the action and words are spliced against each other without links, recreating the sensation of not having time to think.

6 Now show the bottom section of the OHT and ask pupils in pairs to rewrite the paragraph in short sentences that would recreate the breathless panic of the situation.

7 Share and compare contributions, rewarding pupils who break the paragraph into effective short sentences.

H3 Long easy sentences 1

AIM:	To consider the effect of writing in long sentences

YOU WILL NEED:
▶ OHT H3.1

1 Remind pupils that in the last starter they looked at short breathless sentences which communicated panic and excitement.

2 Show OHT H3.1 and explain that these sentences are, by contrast, long and slow. But why have the writers chosen a long slow sentence? Read aloud the sentences one by one in a slow, easy delivery and invite pupils to comment on the effect. Look for the responses:
  - *From a tourist brochure*: to emphasise the relaxation of the holiday.
  - *Chocolate bar wrapper*: to emphasise the luxury and care that has been taken to assemble the product.
  - *Book blurb*: to suggest the large amount that is being offered, and the range of choice available.
  - *Extract from a novel*: to reflect Peter's stream of consciousness.
  - *An in-flight magazine* to reassure nervous passengers and to calm nerves.

3   Ask pupils to generalise about the effect of long slow sentences. Look for these responses:

- It slows down the reading and suggests calm and control.
- A long sentence implies a natural move between one action and the next, taking the reader through a series of events.

Long easy sentences link two or three ideas together, for example the pool, the seashore and dreams in the tourist brochure. Ideas of this kind are often linked with the word 'and'.

H4 Long easy sentences 2

AIM: To consider the effect of writing in long sentences

YOU WILL NEED:

▶ OHT H4.1

1   Remind pupils about their conclusions at the end of the last starter.

2   Show OHT H4.1 and ask pupils to suggest ways of rewriting the first example into long easy sentences which will be more fitting for the subject matter. Discuss options, take suggestions and amend on the OHT as you go. Think aloud about choices.

Draw out:

- The value of connectives.
- How longer sentences allow you to shorten the content overall, and can sound less cumbersome.
- The importance of not over-extending a sentence to the point where you can't remember how it started.

3   Now ask pupils in twos or threes to have a go at the next one, then take suggestions. Comment on effective solutions.

4   Ask pupils to work individually on the third example. In this way, they will learn to apply the approach in the context of their own composition.

H5 Leaving the best till last

AIM: To illustrate the effect of keeping the reader waiting for vital information

YOU WILL NEED:

▶ OHT H5.1

▶ OHT H5.2

1   Show OHT H5.1 and ask pupils to pinpoint the part of the sentence where the surprise, punchline or impact lies. Look for the answer: close to the end.

2 Now ask why the writer might have left it to the end. Look for the responses:

- *Magic trick*: to startle the reader and give a flourish.
- *An advert*: to inspire a thrill and wonder at the size of the prize.
- *Julius Caesar*: the three statements lead to a climax, emphasising the easier and daring of the act.
- *Story*: to withhold from the reader the fact that it is lost for so long. It makes the loss more sudden and absolute.

3 Ask pupils to generalise about why writers might leave the best till last. Look for the responses:

- To lead up to and end on a climax.
- To create a surprise or a punchline.
- To make the reader wait, on tenterhooks.

4 Now show OHT H5.2 and ask pupils how each sentence could be reorganised to put a punch at the end. First identify which element could become the punchline and underline it. Put an arrow to locate it at the end. Then play aloud with the wording to make it work.

5 After one or two, let the groups generate the new sentences and you lead the discussion. By the end, you encourage pupils to work individually so that they apply it in their own composition.

H6 Paragraph endings 1

AIM:	To outline the different uses of paragraph endings

YOU WILL NEED:

▶ OHT H6.1

1 Show OHT H6.1 and take pupils through the paragraphs, asking them how the final line is used, e.g. to surprise, summarise, round off.

2 Take suggestions, rewarding good observations. Look for the following responses:

- *Gliders*: a conclusion to events that is also a punchline, because it deflates the high expectations raised in the paragraph.
- *Train*: a classical summarising sentence which recaps the event and draws out its significance.
- *Moon*: a carefully scripted moment. The metaphor in the final line is set off by the literal everyday actions which precede it. Here is the culmination of a paragraph which is also meant as the culmination of human endeavour!
- *Blurb*: the paragraph trails off, inviting the reader to predict and anticipate events, and thus induce a desire to read the book.

3 Draw out the different uses of last lines to:

- summarise
- surprise
- draw a conclusion
- bring to a climax
- draw out significance
- end a sequence
- keep the reader waiting
- create a sense of ending.

H7 Paragraph endings 2

AIM: To outline the different uses of paragraph endings

YOU WILL NEED:
▶ OHT H7.1

1 Show the first paragraph on H7.1. Ask pupils to consider which sentence they should put at the end if they wanted to give it a punchy ending. Look for the response: 'We have become too busy!' It both summarises the paragraph and gives an exclamation to close on.

2 Move on to the second paragraph and this time ask pupils to provide a new conclusion by adding another sentence to round off the paragraph with a sense of wonder, e.g. 'Little has changed in 200 years!' Reward good attempts.

3 Move on to the notes in the bottom section and ask the class to jot down in twos or threes a short paragraph using the information, but with an ending that will impress the reader with the glamour of fire engines. Reward good attempts.

H8 Paragraph rhythm 1

AIM: To illustrate how sentence length can contribute to meaning in a paragraph

YOU WILL NEED:
▶ OHT H8.1

1 Show OHT H8.1 and ask pupils to look closely at the length of sentences in the first paragraph. Pose the question: Why has the writer chosen to use shorter ones in some places and longer ones in others? Allow 1 minute.

2 Take answers, rewarding good observation. Look for these responses:
- Long sentences to imply a relaxed, controlled or extended experience.
- Short sentence to be curt, direct or shocking, and also to suggest plenty, because it sounds like a list.

3 Repeat with the other two paragraphs. Point out the variety, the rhythm and pace which keep the reader's interest. Look especially at the arresting line 'He knew' in the third example.

4 Ask pupils in pairs to select a product to promote. For example: trainers, a computer magazine or computer game, a fanzine, a pizza, a youth club, a holiday.

5 Ask them to write a short paragraph of advertising text using a mix of long and short sentences appropriately.

H9 Paragraph rhythm 2

AIM: To illustrate how sentence length can contribute to meaning in a paragraph

YOU WILL NEED:
▶ OHT H9.1
▶ Handout H9.2, enough for one each.

1 Show OHT H9.1 and focus on the first paragraph. Pose the question: Why are some sentences short and some long? Allow 30 seconds for pair discussion then take responses. Look for the answer that the short sentences give an urgent, insistent feel and a sense of an overwhelming number of benefits.

2 Move on to the other paragraphs and draw out their rhythms and variations and how these tie up with the meanings intended.

3 Distribute Handout H9.2 and ask pupils to rewrite the first of the two passages using long and short sentences to vary the rhythm and pace, and give impact where it is needed. If they find this difficult, they should focus on simplifying the repeated phrases, or those which are uninteresting. Pupils may add new phrases if it helps them.

4 Ask a pupil to read aloud a successful offering and comment positively on the way sentence length has been manipulated for effect and variety.

5 In the next starter, ask pupils to work in twos or threes on the second paragraph of Handout H9.2. In taking examples, ask pupils to explain their thinking – how they chose to use short and long sentences and what effect they hoped for.

I1 Great things about writing

AIM: To highlight the unique properties of writing in contrast with speech

YOU WILL NEED:

▶ OHT I1.1

▶ Handout I1.2

1 Show OHT I1.1 and ask pupils to consider the difference between speech and writing, then come up with the qualities that are special to writing. Give the pupils a few minutes to discuss in pairs.

2 Gather ideas and reward good suggestions. Point out that writing is:

- permanent, unlike talk which is momentary
- visible, e.g. on paper or a screen
- capable of addressing people not there at the time it was created, e.g. unknown or distant audiences
- capable of revision – it can be edited and amended
- punctuated to guide the reader
- creates a sense of context, time and place ('The Briton', 'aged 22', 'Mont Blanc', 'as he was descending…') as it has to explain in full what is obvious when you are there speaking in person
- often uses subordinate clauses to give additional information (as he was…; as he tried…;)
- often formal in contrast to speech.

3 Point out the most obvious of these features of writing in the newspaper article, particularly the way the context is filled out, e.g. the nationality, the place, the distance he fell. Point out the subordinate clause 'as he was…'. Some pupils may identify the passive 'is believed to have…' which tends not to occur in speech.

4 Show OHT I1.2 ask pupils in pairs to discuss which of the eight features of writing given above can be detected in each extract. Allow two minutes.

5 Take feedback. Reward good observations. Point out the references to time, place and action in the first extract. Emphasise the way the context is created in the second extract – through incidental details, 'We knew…', 'Everyone wanted…', 'Sometimes you'd…'.

12 Great things about speech

AIM: To highlight the unique properties of speech contrasted with writing

YOU WILL NEED:

▶ OHT I1.1

▶ OHT I2.1

▶ OHT I2.2

1 Show OHT I1.1 and pose the question: Name five great things that are true of speaking but are not true of writing. Allow 2 minutes for this activity.

2 If the pupils find this hard, point out the hesitations, the way that one line overlaps with another, the way that specific details are not stated, but understood between speakers. You can also remind them to look at their list from the last starter (Great things about writing) and consider them from another perspective.

3 Take feedback, rewarding good observations. Draw out that way that talk:

- is spontaneous and requires little planning
- is quicker than writing
- benefits from gesture, tone, facial expression, emphasis and timing in a way that writing does not
- means that the speakers can often see each other and know when the other person understands what has been said
- is less formal than writing and contains contractions (e.g. 'wasn't' for 'was not', etc.)
- is momentary – it relies on memory
- is more easily shared than writing – discussion is a co operative effort.

4 Distribute OHT I2.1 and ask pupils to identify these features. Allow 2 minutes.

5 Take feedback. Reward good observations. Point out:

- How the speakers construct the conversation together in the first example, with the listener saying 'yes', 'aye' and 'weren't you frightened?' She helps the speaker by showing she understands. The speaker is constructing the conversation moment by moment (i.e. it is unplanned). Notice also the contractions (weren't, didn't).
- How the commentary works without a conversation.

6 Show OHT I2.2 and ask pupils which features they can identify the context: who is speaking and where the speakers might be. Draw out the way speaking can be brief when the context is obvious. In writing, all this has to be filled in.

13 Appropriateness in speech and writing 1

AIM: To define which language features are most appropriate in speech and writing

YOU WILL NEED:

▶ OHT I3.1

1 Show OHT I3.1 and ask pupils to say why we can be sure this was originally spoken? Draw out:

- The repetition.
- The long sentences.
- The story-telling (historic) present tense, e.g. He hears this noise.
- The emphases, e.g. really.
- The use of 'this'.
- Phatic 'fillers', e.g. Well, so.
- Informal contractions, e.g. 'cos.

2 Ask pupils to help you to convert the piece into written story form and take them through deleting and amending as necessary. As well as dealing with the points above, you need also to emphasise the need for written narrative to build interest and tension when there is no speaker there to animate the story. You could encourage, for example, the use of more effective words than 'getting', 'really' and 'and'. Explain also that more detail in terms of setting and character could help. Discuss the hints that a writer might include to make the reader anticipate what comes next.

14 Appropriateness in speech and writing 2

AIM: To define which language features are most appropriate in speech and writing

YOU WILL NEED:

▶ OHT I4.1
▶ OHT I4.2

1 Show OHT I4.1 and ask pupils to sort out which ones are taken from an oral news bulletin and which from a written newspaper, and which could be either.

2 Take feedback and ask pupils to identify the tell-tale features of oral and written language. Draw out:

- The use of first person in the oral report.
- The way speakers can offer instant updates where as writing takes more time.

- The way speech assumes you can see the obvious, e.g. 'It happened here' assumes you can see where.
- The way the writing contextualises the events, e.g. by referring to time and place.
- The way writing can use visual devices such as capital letters and punctuation marks (e.g. exclamation marks).

3 Show OHT I4.2 and ask pupils to try saying the extracts as if they were casual parts of everyday speech. Then ask them to suggest how they could be changed to make it possible. For example:

- The specialised vocabulary may be explained or simplified.
- The sentences may be shortened and made into several simple sentences.
- Also, the speaker would constantly be checking to see whether the listener had understood what was said. In writing, this moment-by-moment checking is impossible because the audience is not present.

I5 Agreement

AIM:	To explain agreement

YOU WILL NEED:

▶ OHT I5.1

1 Show OHT I5.1 and pose the question: How could the passage be improved? Allow 1 minute for the pupils to work in pairs. Before taking feedback, lead in to the second and more important question: What is the underlying problem? What do all the errors have in common? Allow 30 seconds.

2 Now take feedback. Look for the response that the subject, verbs and tenses do not agree.

3 Use examples to illustrate the point:

- In this passage, the tenses are inconsistent and need to agree, e.g. 'get' and 'wash' are in the present, while 'tied' and 'made' are in the past.
- Notice also the lack of agreement in the singulars and plurals: 'are' and 'that', which should be either: 'What are those?' or 'What is that?'

4 Introduce the term *agreement* and its alternative *concord*. Also introduce the word *consistency*. It is useful in describing the need to maintain the prevailing tense. Although tenses can vary as the narrator refers to past, present and future events, there is a need to maintain a consistent or default time frame through a text. For example, a narrative that starts with past tense verbs should use this tense consistently, unless there is a specific reason for varying it.

5 Orally, remind pupils that local dialect sometimes has its own particular rules about agreement. Use local examples, e.g. The Northern 'I were' or the southern 'we was' or the use of the plural verb with the singular pronoun, e.g. 'he say'. Avoid implying that these forms are wrong: they are not. In writing, the wise choice is standard English which will be understood by most audiences, thus making it more appropriate.

16 Formality 1

AIM:	To identify the key features of formal English

YOU WILL NEED:

▶ OHT I6.1

1 Show the top section of OHT I6.1 and explain the three versions of asking to borrow a pen. Ask who the speaker might be addressing: this will get at the way we adapt our language to suit the formality of the relationship between speaker and listener.

2 Explain the notion of formality:

- Formality demands standard English and adherence to conventions.
- Degree of formality reflects authority relationship.
- Markers of politeness are used in more formal situation, e.g. *please, excuse me.*

3 Show the middle section of the OHT and ask the class to match the statements with the categories.

4 Pose the question: How do you know which are more formal and which are less?

5 Take feedback. You can add to your list:

- Absolute authority is sometimes reflected in the use of direct commands.
- Questions and 'thank you' imply that the listener will co-operate. It suggests an equal rather than an authority relationship, and can be used as a polite command. You could ask pupils for examples of questions which are really commands. (Teachers often do this, e.g. Sally, would you put your chewing gum in the bin now, please?)

6 Show the bottom section of OHT I6.1 and ask for examples of the following versions of the statements:

- formal (e.g. headteacher or distant relative)
- less formal (e.g. mother or father)
- informal (e.g. friend).

17 Formality 2

AIM: To identify the key features of formal English

YOU WILL NEED;

▶ OHT I7.1

▶ Handout I7.2

1 Show OHT I7.1 and pose the question: How could these be rephrased to be more informal for home fans? Allow 1 minute for this.

2 Take feedback and reward good attempts. Ask pupils to generalise about the type of amendments they made. Draw out useful strategies such as:

● reconstructing the sentences so they are no longer commands

● introducing terms of politeness, e.g. *please*

● adding in explanations or introductions to avoid bluntness.

3 Distribute Handout I7.2 and ask pupils to arrange the three extracts in order of formality. Allow about a minute before posing the key question: How did you know? What are the tell-tale signs of formality?

4 Point out the casual opening of 'Hi!', the 'OK' and the 'only joking' of the magazine article. These are features of speech which we associate with informal writing. Notice also how prominent the people are here; the editorial team is mentioned by name, what they do and how they work. Point out that people are not mentioned in the information article, where 'plants…have just taken root…'. Only one example of informal style is to be found here, and it is with the word 'posh' to describe Chanel No 5 perfume. In the rules for a Competition, notice the imperative or command verb, the lack of a second person 'you' and the pared-down language.

18 Formality 3

AIM: To identify the key features of formal English

YOU WILL NEED:

▶ OHT I8.1 cut into strips, a sentence on each strip

▶ OHT I8.2

1 Place the sentence strips from OHT I8.1 randomly on the projector and ask pupils to help you place them in order of formality, with the most formal at the top. (If you have time, you could give them paper versions of this activity to do on the desk top prior to discussion.)

2 As you take suggestions, ask them why they have placed particular statements where they are. Draw out the features of formality and informality already discussed in starter I6. Emphasise that in speech, formality is created through the context of who is speaking, where and to whom. In writing, the formality is created in other ways by using standard English, specialised vocabulary, the full exposition of context and the provision of additional information in subordinate clauses.

3 Move on to show OHT I8.2 and explain that this is the verbal content of a chocolate bar wrapper. Presentation devices have been removed to allow them to focus on the language. Ask pupils to identify the different degrees of formality on the bar and to account for them. Draw out:

- The informality of the advertising elements: the aim is to establish a non-intimidating relationship with potential buyers.
- The way the advertising draws on oral language, popular terminology (*funky*), and unconventional spelling (*Xploder*).
- The minimalism and formality of the factual information.
- The use of imperative verbs for formality, or the absence of any verb.

Section J: Other types of non-fiction

J1 Text types 1

AIM :	To identify the main features of the basic text types

YOU WILL NEED:

▶ J1.1 as an OHT

▶ J1.1 as a set of word cards, enough for one between two or three

▶ Cards J1.2 cut up into strips enough for one set between two or three

1 Show OHT J1.1 to remind pupils of the different text types. They should be familiar with these from previous teaching, but seek or provide an example of each text type for them:

> Instruction – recipes
>
> Explanation – rain cycle
>
> Recount – report of school field trip
>
> Information – encyclopaedia entry
>
> Persuasion – advertising
>
> Discursive writing – review of a controversial issue
>
> Analysis – critique of a poem
>
> Evaluation – evaluation of DT project.

2 Ask them to spread out the word cards (J1.1) and sentence strips (J1.2) and explain that there are two examples of each text type in the set. Their task is to sort them within 3 minutes. Warn them that you are going to ask them how they knew which was which.

3 Take feedback, moving down the list of text types on the OHT. As you go, ask for the correct sentences and then ask the respondent to explain the tell-tale signs in the language. You must keep pushing here, as pupils sometimes think it is self-evident and just want to quote the sentence. Your task is to draw attention to the features of the language which are distinctive.

Instructions

I, 0

- Use of imperative verbs, starts with a command.
- Use of sequencing connectives, e.g. next, finally.
- Simple direct language for ease of use on the job.

Explanation

B, G

- The tell-tale word 'how'.
- Use of present tense.

- Use of logical connectives, e.g. because.

Recount

D, N

- Use of past tense.
- Use of 'We' suggests personal recount.
- Use of temporal connectives, e.g. earlier, when.

Information

F, C

- Impersonal and formal.
- Present tense.
- Formal or technical vocabulary.

Persuasion

J, K

- Direct address to reader.
- Emotive language, e.g. cheer.
- Urgent language, e.g. use of exclamation mark.

Discursive writing

L, H

- Connectives for contrast, e.g. whereas, on the other hand.
- Terms of qualification, e.g. some countries, partial evidence, still consider.
- Balanced sentence structures, e.g. Whereas some…many still…

Analysis

E, P

- Vocabulary of analysis and justification, e.g. implication, effective because…
- Impersonal to imply impartial analysis.
- Present tense.

Evaluation

A, M

- Use of qualifications, e.g. generally, quite, but.
- Direct judgements, e.g. well, successful.
- Use of conditionals, e.g. would have been.

J2 Text types 2

AIM: To identify the main features of the basic text types

YOU WILL NEED:

- ▶ J2.1 cut up into cards enough for one set between two or three
- ▶ J2.2 cut up into cards enough for one set between two or three

1 Distribute a complete set of cards to groups of two or three and ask them to match up the text type, features and two examples.

2 For your convenience, the answers have been lined up on sheets J2.1 and J2.2, so you will need to cut these up before handing them out.

J3 Text types 3

AIM: To identify the main features of the basic text types

YOU WILL NEED:

- ▶ OHT J1.1

1 This starter takes the form of a quiz. Arrange pupils into groups of four and put up OHT J1.1 as a prompt.

2 Pose questions:

1. Which text type usually begins each line with an imperative (command) verb?
   Instruction

2. What kind of text type is a book review?
   Evaluation

3. What kind of text type is a discussion about the pros and cons of capital punishment?
   Discursive

4. Which two text types are dominated by temporal (time sequence) connectives such as next, thirdly, finally?
   Instruction
   Recount

5. Which text type is invariably in the past tense?
   Recount

6. Which text type do all sorts of cycles belong to, e.g. life cycle of a bee, the rain cycle, etc.
   Explanation

7. Which text type is most likely to feature emotive language (to stir the emotions)?
   Persuasion

8. Which two text types address the reader directly?
   Persuasion
   Instruction

9. Give three examples of connectives which might be used to draw out contrast in a piece of discursive writing.
   Whereas
   Compared with
   In contrast to
   Unlike
   On the one hand
   On the other hand

10. Which text type would be most likely to feature these causal (cause and effect) connectives:
    resulting in
    because
    therefore
    causing
    consequently
    Explanation

J4 Text types 4

AIM:	To identify the main features of the basic text types

YOU WILL NEED:

▶ Handout J4.1

▶ Eight pieces of A3 paper, for display material on each text type

1 Divide the class into eight groups. Allocate each group a particular text type. (See list on OHT J1.1). Differentiate by allocating appropriate text types to each group.

2 Ask them to list on their display sheet, examples of writing, titles or schoolwork that would be typical of their text type.

3 Distribute Handout J4.1 and ask them to identify the phrases associated with their particular text type and transcribe them onto the display sheet.

4 Ask them to add to the list examples, phrases or whole sentences to illustrate the text type. Encourage them to think of expressions that could be found at the start of their text type, in the middle and at the end.

J5 Giving directions

| AIM: | To identify the language features of effective directions |

YOU WILL NEED:

▶ OHT J5.1

1 Read aloud the first set of instructions at the top of OHT J5.1. Ask the class how effective these are as a set of instructions, and what is wrong with them. Look for the response: lack of specificity.

2 Show the revised instructions on the bottom half of the OHT. Acknowledge right away that they are better – but why? Allow pupils 3 or 4 minutes to devise five or more rules for giving directions. Look for the following ideas:

- Be specific (e.g. road names).
- Keep it simple (easier to follow).
- Mention landmarks (e.g. opposite the shopping centre).
- Give directions (i.e. left, right).
- Estimate distances.
- Use short sentences (easier to remember).
- Use numbers or connectives to sequence the directions.
- Use the imperative (commands, e.g. Turn left).

3 Ask pupils to write directions for their partner, explaining how to get from your classroom to a different place in the school.

4 Pupils swap directions. Their partner evaluates how successful the directions have been.

5 Amend or add to any of the rules, if necessary.

J6 Instructions

| AIM: | To identify the language features of effective instructions |

YOU WILL NEED:

▶ Cards J6.1, enough for one between two

1 Give each pair of pupils a set of cards. The cards contain a set of instructions, which they need to sequence. Allow 2 minutes.

2 Confirm the order of the instructions: title, D, G, C, B, H, I, A, F, E.

3 Then ask pupils to discuss for 2 minutes how they worked out the right order, particularly looking for clues in the language. Draw out:

- The usefulness of separating the instructions into distinct steps or points.

- The use of sequencing connectives, e.g. after this, next, finally.

4   Now allow pupils a further 2 minutes to discuss what makes the instructions useful. Look for the responses:
- Specific suggestions about how you do something, e.g. underlining key ideas, use colours.
- Breaking the process down into manageable chunks.
- Clear layout, easy-to-follow points.
- Being direct and plain, but also friendly and reassuring.

J7 Explanation

AIM: To identify the language features of effective explanations

YOU WILL NEED:

▶ J7.1 as an OHT and as a handout for each pupil
▶ OHT J7.2

1   Distribute Handout J7.1 and also show it as an OHT. Give pupils 2 minutes in pairs to decide:
1. Which one is the explanation.
2. What, then, the other two are.
3. How they know.

2   Take feedback. Look for the response:
A – persuasion
B – information
C – explanation
Help them to identify language features, and then use OHT J7.2 to confirm the main points. Leave it on the OHP.

3   Next ask pupils to return to the handout. Ask them to annotate the handout with the points on OHT J7.2, pointing out examples of where these features are used in the explanation.

4   As an extension, ask pupils to highlight points in paragraphs A and B in a different colour which signal that these are not explanations, e.g. use of emotive language.

J8 Recount

AIM: To identify the language features of effective recounts

YOU WILL NEED:

▶ J8.1 as an OHT and as a handout for each pupil

▶ OHT J8.2

1 Distribute Handout J8.1 and explain immediately that it is an example of a recount. Ask or remind pupils that a recount is a retelling of a past event. Read the recount.

2 Now show OHT J8.2 which lists some of the common characteristics of a written recount. The task is for pupils to annotate their handouts with these features by making margin notes. Allow 5 minutes.

3 Use an OHT of J8.1 to allow you to gather contributions for pupils who have not, for example, spotted all the connectives.

J9 Persuasion

AIM: To identify the language features of effective persuasive writing

YOU WILL NEED:

▶ J9.1 as an OHT and as a handout for each pupil

▶ OHT J9.2

1 Distribute Handout J9.1 and explain immediately that it is an example of persuasive writing: a leaflet distributed by the RSPCA. Read the text aloud.

2 Ask pupils what effect it has on the reader. Clearly the subject matter is intensely affecting. Allow pupils time to comment on its contents.

3 When their first reactions have been explored, ask the class in what way the information is written to ensure a sympathetic reaction.

4 Now show OHT J9.2 which lists some of the common characteristics of persuasive writing. Remind pupils that persuasive writing is designed to appeal directly to the reader because it wants something such as approval, money or commitment.

5 Ask the class to mention some other types of persuasive writing, e.g. manifestoes, advertisements, charity appeals, political causes, campaigns.

6 The task is for pupils to annotate their handouts with as many of these features as they can find by making margin notes on J9.1. Allow 5 minutes.

7 Use an OHT of J9.1 to point to examples in the feedback though you need to be aware that the print may be too small to read in detail.

J10 Analysis

AIM	To identify the language features of effective analysis

YOU WILL NEED:
- ▶ Handout J10.1 for each pupil
- ▶ OHT J10.2

1 Distribute Handout J10.1 and acknowledge immediately that pupils are looking at two successful pieces of analysis.

2 Ask pupils what 'analysis' means. Look for the response: Analysis is a considered interpretation of evidence such as a text or data.

3 Ask pupils to spend 5 minutes studying the two examples and to come up with a list of typical features of analytic writing.

4 After a few minutes, take responses. Look for the following suggestions:
- Examples are cited as evidence, e.g. quotations, figures.
- Written in third person to sound rational and unbiased.
- Formal tone adopted.
- The paragraph structure of 'point – example – conclusion' is often adopted to present and explain points.
- Connectives are used to direct the reader through the logic of the presentation, e.g. 'similarly', 'also', 'particularly'.
- Present tense.

5 Show OHT J10.2 and acknowledge immediately that this is an example of a poor analysis. Ask pupils to discuss in pairs what the writer has done wrong and how it could be improved. Look for:
- The inappropriate use of the first person.
- It describes but does not analyse what is in the poem.
- It does not explain how the effects have been achieved.
- It uses the past tense.
- Some quotes are unacknowledged, e.g. 'shakes his wet fur…'.

Section A; Starting sentences

A1.1 Different ways of starting sentences

I stayed up even though I was tired.

_____

Even though I was tired, I stayed up.

Walking down the street, I fell over my shoelace.

Before break, I had eaten three bags of crisps.

Silent and forbidding, the school building loomed in front of me.

Quickly and quietly, I slipped under the water.

Besides, he had been really horrible.

Starting with a concession

Although it was raining, I went out.

Despite the fact that _____

_____ ,I_____

_____

Even though _____

_____, she still _____

_____

A3.1 Starting with a reason

Because John was scared, Jenny went on ahead.

As _____.

Since_____.

Subordinators

after	as	before	since
till	until	when	while
where	wherever	if	unless
in case	as long as	supposing	although
though	even if	whereas	whilst
except for	as though	despite	because
for	to	in order to	so as to
like	as if	but for	once
whenever	despite		

TIME	PLACE
ON CONDITION	CONCESSION or RESERVATION
CONTRAST or COMPARISON	EXCEPTION
REASON or PURPOSE	

A5.1 Starting with 'Being'

John was tired and went to sleep.

Because he was tired, John went to sleep.

Because John was tired, he went to sleep.

Being tired John went to sleep.

Being tired, John went to sleep.

Being scared, John hid under the bed.

Starting with other -ing verbs

Walking slowly, John recalled a dream.

Looking warily from side to side Jenny crept down the corridor.

Walking into the room, the teacher gave the pupils a huge smile.

_____ing _____, Jenny turned a

ghostly shade of white.

Turning towards the door in fear, John _____

_____.

A7.1 Starting with a preposition

At the mouth of the cave, Karim hesitated.

Over in the garage, Phil was arguing with Jenny.

In the sewers, rats were already gathering.

Karim hesitated at the mouth of the cave.

Phil was arguing with Jenny in the garage.

Rats were already gathering in the sewers.

Different ways of starting the same sentence 1

The prisoner was crying in his cell.

In his cell, the prisoner was crying.

The prisoner in his cell was crying.

_____

The thief was creeping along the road.

_____

down the alley

the cybernaut was creaking

with a lasergun in his hand

A10.1 **Different ways of starting the same sentence 2**

when he had finished eating

John put on his frogman suit

When he had finished eating, John put on his frogman suit.

John put on his frogman suit when he had finished eating.

John, when he had finished eating, put on his frogman suit.

Jenny entered the catacombs

her heart pounding against her ribs

holding her torch in trembling hands

Section B: Asides and extras

B1.1 Expanding nouns 1

The boy walked down the street.

The sad, melancholy, unhappy boy walked down the dark, dismal, dreary street.

Jenny was angry and upset.

Angry and upset, Jenny stormed out of the room.

Jenny stormed out of the room, angry and upset.

Jenny stormed out of the room. As the door closed, a brief smile appeared on her lips.

Expanding nouns 1

John staggered down the street.

John was really cross. He came in with an angry look on his face. Jenny was really surprised when she saw how mad he was.

oht

B2.1 Expanding nouns 2

The boy in the ragged jumper walked down the street.

_____

Horror

Romance

Adventure

Science fiction

Mystery

Police story

Comedy

Expanding verbs

Jenny ran.

Wildly Jenny ran.

Jenny ran down the lonely street.

John stared.

The girl looked through the window.

^ The ^ girl ^ looked ^ through the ^ window ^.

Fearfully, the pale girl with straggling hair looked in despair through the grimy window of the secluded castle.

The man was talking in the phone box.

B4.1 Dropping an extra clause into a sentence

Jenny	entered	the	room	,
who was shaking with fear				,
although she was scared				,
feeling full of confidence				,

.	.

John	ran	off
although he knew he should stay		
fearing the worst		,
who was very scared		,

Comma splicing

John had been on holiday to Greece, Jenny thought it was unfair. He was all brown, he looked fit and healthy, she looked all weedy and pale in comparison. And he still had loads of money left.

B6.1 Commas

I hate all boys who are idiots.

I hate all boys, who are idiots.

All girls who are boring revolt me.

All girls, who are boring, revolt me.

I went home, had my tea, watched television and threw my homework down the toilet.

Jenny, my elder sister, tells lies.

Although he was there, John said nothing.

John, however, said nothing.

Commas

1 To separate items in a list

I went home, had my tea, watched television and threw my homework down the toilet.

2 To drop in extra information

Jenny, my elder sister, tells lies.

3 To separate subordinate from main clauses

Although he was there, John said nothing.

Jenny, who was also afraid, remained silent.

4 To separate connectives from the rest of the sentence

John, however, said nothing.

5 To generalise about groups of people

All girls, who are boring, revolt me.

B7.1 The complex sentence

Jenny was on the phone to her gang. John was crying on his bed.

_____

While Jenny was on the phone to her gang John was crying on his bed.

_____

1 Jenny ran down the street. She looked behind her. She was worried about what had just happened at home.

2 Some people think that cloning animals is wrong. They think it's going against nature. They are not always fully informed about the facts.

3 Evacuation began as soon as the war started. Many children returned home quite soon. Bombing did not start as quickly as everyone had expected.

Revision

1   Combine these four simple sentences into no more than two
    new sentences.

    **I walked down the street. Lights came on in several windows. I felt a
    shiver of fear. I walked on.**

    Write here:

2   Rewrite this sentence as instructed at each stage:
    a) Underline the main clause:

    As I watched, the boys fell over.

    b) Underline the subordinate clause:

    As I watched, the boys fell over.

    c) Circle the conjunction or joining word which links the two
    clauses together:

    As I watched, the boys fell over.

    d) Rewrite the sentence here, changing the verb in the main clause:

    e) Rewrite the sentence here, changing the verb in the subordinate
    clause:

    f) Rewrite the sentence, changing the order of the clauses and
    inserting commas if necessary:

    g) Change the order of the clauses again to a new position, inserting
    commas if necessary:

    h) Rewrite the sentence, changing the conjunction:

    i) Separate the sentences into two simple sentences:

    j) Add a new clause to the sentence:

Section C: Clarifying meaning

C1.1 Ambiguity 1

Newspaper headlines

Giant waves down funnel

Boy held by teachers over fire.

Examples from jokes:

How do you make a cheese roll?
Push it down hill.

Ambiguity 1

John was stuck in the jam for three hours.

Police hold man in violin case.

Computer games for sale by a man going abroad in a plastic box with a joystick.

They can fish.

They are cooking apples.

General Flies Back To Front.

The Prime Minister thanked the people he had fought with all his life.

He took two aspirin tablets to cure his headache which made him feel much better.

We decided to pack the car and take a long trip.

He told him he had been selected to play.

Police ordered to stop sleeping in doorways.

The problem with pronouns

She told her she had been chosen to run.

When they woke they were all gone.

My uncle told the shopkeeper that he had made a mistake.

If the baby doesn't thrive on fresh milk, boil it.

Charlie Brown told Pigpen he had won the competition.

Resolving ambiguity with sensible sequencing

1   There is a notice board where pupils can pin the titles of their recommended books in our classroom.

2   We had a pre-match sandwich and recalled the old games and the stories of Stanley Matthews who played for Stoke and spent a great deal of time waiting for the bus.

3   He could hear a lot of conversation about him.

4   Please state the time when the patient was sent to bed and totally incapacitated by your instructions.

5   Check here to find what computer hardware and memory you need to use.

Crazy Headlines

<u>A</u>tom <u>b</u>omb <u>c</u>rushed <u>D</u>angermouse

<u>E</u>merald <u>F</u>ountain <u>g</u>rasped <u>H</u>ercules.

<u>I</u>.............. <u>J</u>.............. <u>K</u>.............. <u>L</u>..............

Hiding the agent

- The book was read.

- The door was opened.

- The pizza was eaten.

- The pop star was met at the station.

- City centre was wrecked.

- The bank was robbed.

- The science experiment was set up.

- The school was rewarded.

- The galaxy Andromeda was photographed.

- The bridge was completed in July.

- The football team was considered the best in the league.

- Several witnesses saw how the dog was injured.

C7.1) Laying the blame

1 The goalkeeper was fouled.

2 The money was stolen.

3 Our car was bumped.

4 The window was smashed.

5 The tennis player was put off her game.

6 The player should be dropped from the team for his poor performance.

7 The player was sent off.

8 The team will be changed.

9 The crowd was disappointed.

10 The penalty was taken.

11 The final whistle was blown.

Laying the blame

Overheard:

- Someone's been injured in the playground.

- The biscuits have all been eaten.

From stories:

- Mrs Tidyheart noticed that dirt had been trodden into the carpet.

- That's it, thought Jenny. I've been lied to once too often!

From newpapers:

- Oldest building to be demolished.

- Burglar shot in bank raid.

Signs:

- Cars parked in reserved bays will be clamped.

- Litter louts will be prosecuted.

- Requests for credit will be refused.

C8.1 Actives, passives and agents

Please, sir, the science lab window by the football field has been broken.

I saved the day.

Enemy ship sunk – 100 dead.

We won the election.

Please, miss, I was pushed over in the playground.

I must go because I am late for an important meeting.

The meeting was delayed.

A tax increase has been announced.

We won the election.

Section D: Time and motion

D1.1 Tenses 1

The bell will go at 3.15pm.

Tomorrow we shall hear the results.

They will be eating supper by the time you get home.

I am going to save my pocket money.

I go to Manchester next Sunday.

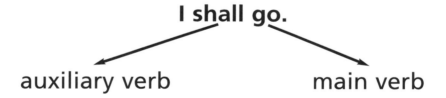

I shall go.

auxiliary verb   main verb

You will obey.

auxiliary verb   main verb

Tenses 2

I started at Midhurst Primary School when I was nine. I had been going to a very small school in Bridlington but my family moved. I have made lots of new friends here and I am learning to swim which I enjoy very much. Next September I will transfer to a secondary school in Brighton. I visited the school once this term and I can't believe how large it is. I am feeling a bit nervous about it. When the bell rang, all the pupils began to move to different rooms for different subjects. I do hope we won't get lost in the first few days.

D2.2 Tenses 2

Cut up the cards.

do hope	can't believe	will transfer
started	am feeling	won't get lost
was	rang	is
moved	enjoy	visited
had been going	have made	began to move

Verb phrases

I am looking forward to my birthday.

I don't know how you put up with me.

Time to get up and go off to your lessons.

D4.2 Verb phrases

put paid	look	look
look	swimming	calm
hand	vote	cheer
switch	turn	wander
make	care	rise
soldier	close	cave
off	on	off
out	for	up
down	in	to
to	to	on
on	up	up
in	for	up

Lonely verbs

The infinitive

We did want *to join* the club.

I am going *to bake* a cake.

They have been *to see* the team leader.

The -ing participle

I am *eating* my dinner.

I was *hoping* to see you tomorrow.

The builders will be *working* here tomorrow.

The -ed participle

I have *typed* the letter for you.

He has *trained* very hard for this race.

We have *made* three attempts at this experiment.

D6.1 Irregular verbs 1

upset	burn	lend	bind	think	stick	creep
spread	mean	build	find	bring	swing	deal
shut	spoil	bend	grind	teach	dig	dream
hurt	deal	spend	wind	catch	strike	feel
cut	learn	buy	fight	sit	keep	bit
send	bind	seek	shine	kneel	put	come
leave	hold	sleep	cost	sting	speed	read
weep	drive	rise	fly	give	run	fall
do	go	make	know	drink	tell	lie
swim	sing	eat	grow	throw	have	say
pay	write	shoot	spring	am	meet	shake
take	stand	bear	sink	see	light	blow

Irregular verbs 2

CHANGE	PRESENT TENSE	PAST TENSE
No change	cut	cut
Just add T	burn	burnt
IND changes to OUND	bind	bound
Change the last D to T	spend	spent
Only the middle vowel changes	rise	rose
End changes to OUGHT	buy	bought
Ending changes to EW	fly	flew
Words that are unique	am	was

D9.1 Changing tenses

Nowadays, I go to the cinema regularly.

I hope it will be a hot day tomorrow.

I feel sick because I have eaten too much.

I can see some people through the window, but I cannot hear what they are saying.

Prevailing tenses

1   Jokes

2   The method section when you write up a scientific experiment

3   The conclusions section of a scientific experiment

4   A history essay

5   Factual information about the natural world e.g. volcanoes

6   A party political manifesto

7   An instruction manual

8   A tourist brochure

9   A match report

10 The morning news

Section E: Speech

E1.1 Ground rules

1 CARTOON

2 SCRIPT

DRACULA   I am expecting some people for dinner, Igor. Is everything prepared?

IGOR   Yes master. I have swept the dungeons, hidden all crosses and stakes and made sure there is no garlic anywhere in the castle.

DRACULA   Good. I am getting hungry. I hope they come soon.

IGOR   I can hear a banging on the door. I think dinner has arrived!

3 PROSE

'I am expecting some people for dinner, Igor. Is everything prepared?' said Dracula.

'Yes master,' Igor replied. 'I have swept the dungeons, hidden all crosses and stakes and made sure there is no garlic anywhere in the castle.'

Dracula said, 'Good. I am getting hungry. I hope they come soon.'

'I can hear a banging on the door. I think dinner has arrived!' exclaimed Igor.

Commas – where exactly do they go?

John asked, 'Why did the beetroot blush?'

'I expect it's because he fancied a date,' replied Jane.

'Actually,' said John, 'it's because he saw the salad dressing.'

E2.2 Commas – where exactly do they go?

'I cannot believe that you have spent all afternoon walking up and down that field,' said Jane.

'What you don't realise,' said Peter, 'is that metal detecting can be very rewarding.'

'I don't think so!' she scoffed.

'A local farmer found some metal trash in his field and it turned out to be worth a fortune,' continued Peter. 'You just have to be patient and keep trying.'

'Have you found anything yet?' Jane asked.

'No,' admitted Peter.

Commas – where exactly do they go?

I cannot believe that you have spent all afternoon walking up and down that field said Jane.

What you don't realise said Peter is that metal detecting can be very rewarding.

I don't think so! she scoffed.

A local farmer found some metal trash in his field which turned out to be worth a fortune continued Peter. You just have to be patient and keep trying.

Have you found anything yet? Jane asked.

No admitted Peter.

E3.1 The speaker tag

The two friends sat down to drink from their cans and began to think of the end of term.

'What are you going to do in the holidays?' asked Clare. 'Do you have any plans?'

'I am going to stay with my cousins for a week,' replied Julie. 'I go every year. What about you?'

'We hire a caravan and drive to the coast. We stay at the same place every year. It's great actually, but I get bored in the car.'

Julie agreed. 'I think the best bit about holidays is being at home and having time to do things. I enjoy that as much as being away.'

'I can't wait,' said Clare.

Alternatives to 'exclaimed'

'Ouch!'

'Halt!'

'You're standing on my toe!'

Section F: Paragraphs

F1.1   Cues to start a new paragraph 1

Ben followed her inside. It took his eyes a while to get used to the gloom, so for the first few seconds he was blinded and deafened. Then he found himself looking at thousands and thousands of chickens in tiny wire cages, stacked from floor to roof, stretching away into the distance.

He remembered the Old Macdonald's Farm picture book he'd had as a kid. One page sprang to mind, a farmyard filled with fat white hens pecking the earth.

These miserable creatures were from a different planet.

He walked down an aisle, horrified. The lank, greasy feathers. The deformed beaks. The sores. The dull, hormone-bloated eyes. And the deafening noise of misery.

Under each cage was a chute leading to a conveyor belt which in turn led to big egg-sorting machines. Next to one of these Ben picked up an egg box from a stack waiting to be filled. On the lid were the words 'Fresh Farm Eggs' with a drawing of a traditional farmyard.

Suddenly the squawks near Ben got even louder. He spun round.

Esmé had opened a cage door and hauled out a chicken, which was trying for the first time in its life to walk.

The Other Facts of Life, Morris Gleitzman

Cues to start a new paragraph 1

Claire Guthrie keeled over and crashed to the kitchen floor. She lay motionless, eyes closed, arms splayed. Instead of sprinting to the phone, ringing an ambulance, sprinting back, giving Claire mouth-to-mouth, weeping, panicking and making silly deals with God, her mother merely sighed and plonked down a steak the size of Tasmania onto the kitchen table in front of Ben. 'Claire' said Di, long-sufferingly. Ben wasn't too worried by his sister's collapse either. He thought she'd held the horrified stare at her plate a couple of seconds too long and one roll of the eyes before going down would have done but at that moment he was more interested in beef than ham. He stared thoughtfully at the two huge steaks steaming on the table. Claire's eyes snapped open and she dragged herself theatrically onto her chair. 'Sorry,' she said, 'it was just too much for me, the sight of three months meals all on the one plate.'

The Other Facts of Life, Morris Gleitzman

F2.1 Cues to start a new paragraph 2

Sayle giggled. "Forgive me, Alex, if I don't believe you," he said. His face was suddenly stone. "And perhaps you forget that I warned you about lying to me."

Mr Grin took a step forward, flipping the knife over so that the blade landed in the flat of his hand.

"I'd like to watch you die," Sayle said. "Unfortunately, I have a pressing engagement in London." He turned to Mr Grin. "You can walk with me to the helicopter. Then come back here and kill the bot. Make it slow. Make it painful. We should have kept back some smallpox for him – but I'm sure you'll think of something much more creative."

He walked to the door, then stopped and turned to Alex.

"Goodbye, Alex. It wasn't a pleasure knowing you. But enjoy your death. And remember, you're only going to be the first…"

The door swung shut. Handcuffed to the chair with the jellyfish floating silently behind him, Alex was left alone.

Stormbreaker, Anthony Horowitz

Cues to start a new paragraph 2

It was the enemy who finally broke. He was less than five metres away, so close that Alex could make out the perspiration on his forehead. Just when it seemed that a crash was inevitable, he twisted his quad and swerved off the path, up on to the embankment. At the same time, he tried to fire his gun. But he was too late. His quad was slanting, tipping over onto two of its wheels, and the shot went wild. The man yelled out. Firing the gun had caused him to lose what little control he had left. He fought with the quad, trying to bring it back on to four wheels. It hit a rock and bounced upwards, landed briefly on the footpath, then continued over the edge of the cliff. Alex had felt the machine rush past him, but he had seen little more than a blur. He had shuddered to a halt and turned round just in time to watch the other quad fly into the air. The man, still screaming, had managed to separate himself from the bike on the way down, but the two of them hit the water at the same moment. The quad sank a few seconds before the man. Who had sent him? It was Nadia Vole who had suggested the walk, but it was Mr Grin who had actually seen him leave. Mr Grin had given the order – he was sure of it. Alex took the quad all the way to the end of the path. The sun was still shining as he walked down into the little fishing village, but he couldn't enjoy it. He was angry with himself because he knew he'd made too many mistakes. He should have been dead by now, he knew. Only luck and a low-voltage electric fence had managed to keep him alive.

Stormbreaker, Anthony Horowitz

F3.1 Paragraph structure 1

A First, you separate the eggs and add the egg whites to the bowl. Then, you whip the egg whites until light and fluffy. After that, you gradually spoon in the castor sugar, beating the mixture further as the sugar is added.

B A volcano is essentially a safety valve. Eruptions are the result of pressures building up in the molten rocks below the surface of the earth. These pressures seek escape through the weak spots in the earth's crust, causing cracks to open and lava to spill out. Violent eruptions are caused when the collection of hot gases at the mouth of the volcano are ignited. The mountain itself is created of molten lava which hardens in the cool air, and thus builds up a raised lip around the mouth of the eruption.

C There is good sense in giving teenagers an allowance instead of pocket money. The first and most important reason is that it gives them first hand experience of managing a budget and this is one of the key skills of adult life. It also allows them the flexibility to spend money on things that they – rather than their parents – want to buy. Even if things go wrong and the money is spent unwisely, then at least they learn to live with their mistakes and spend the money more responsibly in future.

Paragraph structure 2

A Before buying a pet, it is important to think about several aspects of pet ownership. First and most important: do you have the space, equipment and time to care for the pet adequately? Secondly, are your parents happy with your decision to buy a pet? Also, you should consider if you can afford the ongoing costs of keeping your pet.

B To clean the percolator, dissolve the salts into the water tank and heat the element. Just before the water boils, turn off the switch and leave the water to cool. After two hours, empty the tank and rinse it twice with cold water. Finally boil a tank of water and empty it before you use the percolator to make a drink.

C There are several good reasons to abolish the death penalty. Firstly, there are the rights of the individual. It is not our role to deprive others of the right to life and therefore other forms of punishment, such as imprisonment, should be adopted. Secondly, and almost as important in my opinion, is whether the death penalty is always deserved. Too often evidence is uncovered at a later date which causes the earlier trial decision to be overturned. If a man's life has already been ended it is then too late for justice to take place.

D Many rivers in our country are becoming polluted. As a result, a range of species is endangered: fish die, otters lose their food and habitat, and water birds become extinct. The cause of continuing pollution is man's self-centred attitude. He places his needs above those of the environment. However, this attitude cannot be allowed to continue indefinitely; we will realise to our cost that we need to live in harmony with the environment, or we will inevitably leave to our children a wasteland of our own creation.

E When there is competition for a product or service, people shop around for the best deal, and so prices are driven down. Consequently, only the most economic and efficient businesses are able to survive. Over a period of time, the reduced competition means people have less choice and once again this leads to a gradual increase in prices.

F5.1 Paragraph structure 3

A Because wild animals are vulnerable to attack from predators, they tend to stay in groups, and all the herd, including the new-born, have to be able to run away. Thus, the young will usually stand within a few minutes of being born, and soon they take their first steps. In this way nature allows both mother and baby to stay with the herd and gain added protection from predators.

B Travel by air is generally very safe nowadays. The statistics indicate that people are one hundred times less likely to be injured from air accidents than car accidents. For this reason people have no reason to fear travelling by plane.

C The government has introduced a wide-ranging set of options to enable young people to stay on at school and follow asuitable course. There are 'A' level courses for those who wish to continue to university; advanced GNVQ courses for those who may go to university or college; and intermediate GNVQ courses for student who wish to develop practical skills that will allow them to find a job on leaving school. With this choice available, it is easier for 16 year olds to find an appropriate course to study after their GCSE exams.

D Bali is known as the island of the gods. The locals believe that the gods would have inhabited this romantic island were they to live on earth. Bali lives up to its reputation. Its magical sunsets and charming people attract a huge number of visitors.

E Many flowers have special features to ensure pollination. For example, foxgloves have attractive markings at the edge of the flower to guide the insect into the pollen. The insects enter the tube of the flower to gain the pollen. This is evidence of nature's adaptability.

F Exercise is essential for a healthy lifestyle. People who do not exercise are more likely to develop heart disease and suffer from obesity. They are also more likely to suffer from depression. For this reason, doctors recommend some form of exercise at least three times a week.

Paragraph structure 4

Terrapins

Live in fresh water.

Can weigh up to 90 kgs.

Related to tortoises, but have flatter shells.

Breathe air but they can hold their breath for a long time.

150 species of terrapin.

Meat-eaters, catching small fish, etc.

Have been known to hunt ducks.

A small reptile.

Can grow to be 70cms long.

F7.1 Paragraph diagrams 1

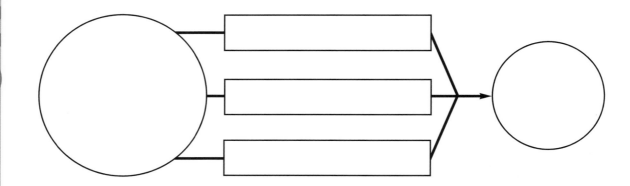

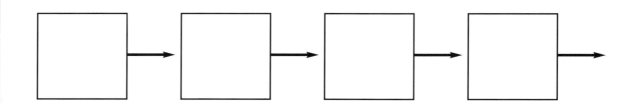

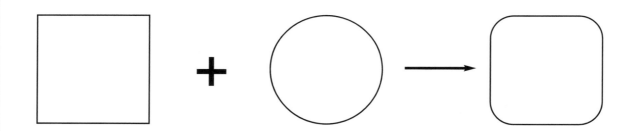

Paragraph diagrams 1

F9.1 Paragraph diagrams 3

A

- At seventeen young people are able to learn to drive a car
- Need to write a theory test first
- Then, after theory test, usually have driving lessons
- Once confident, after eighteenth birthday, may take driving test
- If you pass, receive provisional licence
- After six months, may apply for full driving licence

B

- Tidying your room causes conflict in families
- Untidy bedroom: hated by parents
- Tidying one's room: hated equally by teenagers
- Many battles fought: how often, when, whose responsibility?
- Lucky: any family without this conflict!

C

- Elephants have ivory tusks
- Tusks are very valuable – for jewellery
- Poachers kill elephants to obtain their tusks

D

- Technology affects most people's lives, and has helped to make life easier
- Examples: computers, dishwashers, telephones, medical equipment
- Developing countries strive to develop their technology, to improve the quality of life

Paragraph diagrams 3 (continued)

E

- Ducks, geese and chickens all have down feathers which are very soft
- These feathers are used to make duvets and pillows
- The feathers have different density and availability
- There is a wide variety in price

F

- Fruit and vegetables provide us with vitamins and minerals
- Milk and dairy products give us calcium and vitamins
- Potatoes and starchy food provide the building blocks for our bodies
- Protein is needed to develop connective tissue and feed our brains
- Water is essential as ninety percent of our bodies are made of water
- All these items form a healthy diet and are essential for us to live

G

- If your puppy is ill, you may need to take him to the vet
- The vet may prescribe medicine, such as antibiotics
- The best way to administer this is with a syringe
- Draw fluid into syringe, then squirt down puppy's throat

F11.1 Paragraph composition 2

A
- Increase in number of young musicians
- Lots of talent
- Successful
- More young people have opportunity to follow dreams
- Examples: *Billie Piper, Britney Spears, Westlife*

B
- Mammals have unusual features
- Whales – live in the sea
- Hippopotamuses – live in rivers or estuaries
- Kangaroos – pouches
- Elephants – trunks and tusks
- Giraffes – long necks

C
- Exercise or playing sport:
    - warm up
    - have skills demonstrated
    - coaching
    - practice
    - play
    - debrief

D
- Three social classes: peasants, middle class and privileged landowners
- Desire to overthrow king
- Violence and loss of life
- Establish elected parliament
- French Revolution began in 1789
- Revolution lasted for six years

E
- Buy material and pattern
- Cut out pattern pieces
- Pin pattern to material
- Cut out material
- Tack sections together before machine-stitching
- Stitch all seams
- Hem

Paragraph organisation

LIONS

- Male has longer, more pronounced mane
- Competition for food from scavengers such as jackals and vultures
- Seem lazy – lie in the shade, away from the midday sun
- Lions are skilful predators
- Females hunt
- Females look after young
- Pride has specific area that forms their territory
- Tawny or sandy-coloured coat
- Mane is often darker – almost black
- Short bursts of speed, but cannot run fast for long
- Very strong animals
- Lions live in a pride
- Play-fighting helps teach cubs how to hunt
- Lionesses usually hunt together
- Kill other animals to live
- Cubs are brought up together, as a family, but drink milk from their mother
- Generally live on plains – vast stretches of land
- Males are the 'King' of the pride
- Circle their prey or separate them from the rest of the herd
- Swipe of lioness's paw can break neck of prey
- Usually attack jugular vein in throat
- Cubs are very playful
- Lionesses single out old, ill or young animals to attack
- Other males may challenge the lion for his pride
- Innards of prey supplement water intake

F13.1 Paragraph links and signposts 1

The man went to take the man's dog for a walk. The man called to Toto the dog, and showed Toto's lead. As the man and the dog were leaving the house, the man's daughter explained that the man's daughter would like to join the man and the dog for a walk to the florist. The man's daughter wanted to buy a bouquet of flowers for the man's daughter's aunt, as the man's daughter's aunt was recovering from an operation and the man's daughter planned to visit the man's daughter's aunt later in the evening.

The teacher explained the rules of the game to the pupils. The pupils listened carefully as the pupils were excited about the opportunity to play a new game: water polo. The teacher asked the pupils to repeat the rules to the teacher. The pupils did; most of the pupils had understood the rules, but one of the pupils had not. Therefore, the whole class waited for the teacher to repeat the teacher's explanation and for the confused pupil to show the teacher that the pupil had now understood. The other pupils were frustrated that the pupils were missing valuable time in the swimming pool.

Paragraph links and signposts 2

1
Also
Moreover
Furthermore
Additionally

2
Firstly
Secondly
Thirdly
Finally
Later
Next
Then
After this

3
Similarly
Likewise
By comparison

4
However
On the other hand
In comparison
An opposing view
Alternatively

5
Although
Except for
Other than
If only

6
For example
Such as
For instance

7
Consequently
As a result
So
Hence
Therefore

8
In conclusion
As we have seen
To summarise
In the end
Overall

F14.2 **Paragraph links and signposts 2**

My mother was angry with me.

I had not told her I was going to be late.

She was worried.

Our match was postponed.

We were disappointed.

We were looking forward to a challenging game.

We wanted to prove ourselves against strong opponents.

A hippopotamus is commonly called a hippo.

They are unusual mammals because they live in water.

They do not eat fish.

They eat grass at the side of the river.

Paragraph links and signposts 3

Puppies make wonderful pets. You can take a puppy for a walk. You can play games with it. Puppies are friendly. They are affectionate. They will cuddle up to you when you are feeling sad. You have to look after your puppy well. This requires time and money. He will need regular exercise. He will need the correct food and sufficient fresh water each day. You will have to take him to the vet to receive his injections. You do not want him to get ill.

F15.2 Paragraph links and signposts 3

Swimming is a wonderful sport. Being able to swim could save your life in an emergency. Your body is supported in the water. This is unlike running. No pressure is placed on any of your joints. This means you are likely to have few injuries. The most difficult part of learning to swim is conquering your fear of the water. It is very relaxing, like many other forms of exercise. You focus on the exercise you are doing, not your problems, which is a good way to reduce stress.

Key sentences

Lions are majestic animals. In stories, they are often referred to as Kings among other animals. This term is appropriate as they are dominant predators, killing their prey with ease.

Lions live in a pride, and each pride dominates a large area. The male lion is the leader of the pride, but the females do the majority of the work, hunting and looking after the young cubs. After a kill it is generally the lion that eats first, while the lionesses have to wait their turn! Because prides are large, with control over large stretches of land, other males sometimes challenge the lion for control of his pride.

The female lionesses are skilful hunters. They tend to hunt together and use clever tactics to catch their prey. For example, they may encircle their prey, or separate them from the rest of the herd. They also tend to choose the old, ill or young animals to attack because they are weaker and more vulnerable. Although lions are strong they are unable to run for long periods, so they have to rely on tactics and skill to outwit their prey. A sideways swipe from a lioness's paw can break an animal's neck. Once the animal is killed, the pride eats quickly before the other predators such as jackals and vultures arrive to share the kill.

Hunting is vital to the success of a pride, so young cubs need to learn to hunt and fight successfully. Much of the play-fighting that occurs between cubs is preparation for their role as hunters later.

Lions have tawny or sandy-coloured coats, and thus they are well camouflaged amongst the dry, sandy plains and long grass in Africa. They seem lazy, and are often seen lying in the shade during the heat of the midday sun, but they are capable of short bursts of speed when necessary. They tend to be more active in the early mornings or late afternoons when it is slightly cooler.

F17.1 Grabbing the reader's attention in the first line

'When the doorbell rings at three in the morning, it's never good news.'
[*Stormbreaker*, Anthony Horowitz]

'Macy dashed out of the high school, filled with the energy of Friday afternoon.'
[*Burning up*, Caroline B. Cooney]

'I found him in the garage on a Sunday afternoon.'
[*Skellig*, David Almond]

'The last minutes of the last lesson of the last day of term were ticking away, and Martin Turner could not wait to be set free.'
[*Face*, Benjamin Zephaniah]

'Greg was being watched again.'
[*The Protectors*, Pete Johnson]

'On the day her life changed forever, Sky woke early.'
[*Throwaways*, Ian Strachan]

'Palm trees don't like the cold.'
[*Daz 4 Zoe*, Robert Swindells]

'I have a stone that looks like a snake: all curled up.'
[*The Snake-stone*, Berlie Doherty]

'I keep thinking that I have a tunnel in my chest.'
[*After the First Death*, Robert Cormier]

'A trickle of late-afternoon passengers came out of the Underground at Oakwood, waving seasons and throwing tickets into the empty collector's cabin.'
[*Running Scared*, Bernard Ashley]

'Jo should have known better.'
[*Waiting for Anya*, Michael Morpugo]

'The bike was a dare – not by anyone else, because he was alone, but a dare to himself.'
[*Collision Course*, Nigel Hinton]

'Maybe we all want to burn off across the horizon, into space, perhaps, to take off into some unknown territory and meet ourselves out there.'
[*Dear Nobody*, Berlie Doherty]

Punchline conclusions 1

Then I swung up and out, up through my arms, up out of my waiting stance, till only the air was holding me. I spun and spun again, another half spin. I was a curled-up snake falling like a stone out of the sky. And then I reached out and down, full stretch, long and taut and swift, and ripped clean through the water.

I was home.

The Snake-stone, Berlie Doherty

Now he had reached the dead end, and there was no more running to be done. He had to turn and let his parents see that the innocent Ray had died years ago and that this was what he was. In the same way that the accident, and now his discovery, had seemed to consist of various elements heading on a collision course, what his parents were having to face about their son was inevitable, too. All people move through their lives thinking that they knew where they were going but they couldn't see what events were heading in their direction to alter their course or bring it to a sudden end.

When he turned into his road, the police car was parked outside his house.

Collision Course, Nigel Hinton

F19.1 Punchline conclusions 2

And Mr Sibley had known after all where to start finding allies, because Grace nodded, and so did Lindsay, and the three of them went down the hall together.

There were fires to put out.

Burning up, Caroline B. Cooney

He turned his back on Alex and climbed into the helicopter cabin. The blades started up and a few seconds later the helicopter rose back into the air. For a moment it hovered at the side of the building. Behind the glass, Yassen raised his hand. A gesture of friendship? A salute? Alex raised his hand. The helicopter spun away.

Alex stood where he was, watching it, until it had disappeared in the dying light.

Stormbreaker, Anthony Horowitz

After a few steps Chip said, 'My feet hurt.'

Sky turned and was about to shout at him until she realised he was smiling.

'Only kidding,' he said, quietly sneaking his hand into hers as they walked side by side up the road.

Throwaways, Ian Strachan

Today my nan came to the house. It wasn't easy for her to come, I know that. We sat in the front room together; Nan on the hard chair, Mum by the window, me in the low nursing-chair with Amy. Nan didn't say much, but then, you wouldn't expect her to. She just watched me in that sad, nodding way of hers. When I finished feeding Amy and was just about to put her down, all milky-sweet and sleepy, Mum came over and took her from me. She just kissed her, the way she does, and then she walked back across the room and put her in Nan's arms.

It was as though Amy was a fine thread being drawn through a garment, mending tears.

Dear Nobody, Berlie Doherty

handout

Section G: The shape of writing

G1.1 Signposts

Circuses

Circuses are popular for a variety of reasons. They are an excellent form of entertainment, appealing to the whole family. For example, they have magicians, to enchant the audience; clowns, for laughter, tricks and fun; animals to perform tricks; and trapeze artists, who impress with their gymnastic skill.

Looking beyond the glamour of the performance, however, some people are critical of what they offer. The humour of the clowns can be cruel, and the treatment of animals humiliating.

Furthermore, opponents of circuses have real concerns about the living conditions and treatment of the animals. Many circus animals are caged in confined and unnatural environments. They were not created to perform tricks in order to earn rewards or treats, and they are certainly not intended to perform in front of large noisy audiences. It is these aspects of the circus that people who defend the rights of animals find difficult to support.

On the other hand, supporters commend the close bonds that develop between animals and their trainers. Moreover, they claim that circuses help to conserve endangered species.

To sum up, circuses have their critics, but despite this a large number of people enjoy attending circus performances.

Layout

G2.2 Layout

Organising argument 1

What the issue is	
The main point FOR	The main point AGAINST
Another point FOR	Another point AGAINST
Another point FOR	Another point AGAINST
A summing up FOR	A summing up AGAINST
Summary of argument	Conclusion

G4.1 Organising argument 2

What the issue is	
The main point FOR	
The main point AGAINST	
Another point FOR	
Another point AGAINST	
A summing up FOR	
A summing up AGAINST	
Summary of argument	
Conclusion	

Organising information

BRAZIL

A brief introduction to Brazil, outlining the main details about the country's geography or environment, their imports and exports, and the favourite recreational activities.

Key facts

Location: Brazil is the largest country in South America.
Capital: Rio de Janiero.
Official language: Portuguese
Main religion: Catholic

Geographical features

a) The Amazon
The Amazon consists of swamps, floodplains and tropical rainforests. Because of the density of the vegetation, much of the territory is still unexplored.

b) The highlands
The highlands are an area that has been eroded over thousands of years. The landscape is diverse, with mountains and rivers, prairies and forests.

c) The coastline
The extensive coastline has lots of natural harbours and beaches.

Trade

Exports
Brazil is the world's largest producer of coffee and orange juice concentrate. Furthermore, they are the second largest producer of soya beans. Additionally, Brazil exports iron ore, footwear and motor-vehicle parts.

Imports
Brazil needs to import crude oil, coal, chemical products, some food [particularly wheat] and manufactured goods.

G5.1 Organising information continued

Environmental issues

- Deforestation
- Water pollution in urban areas
- Traffic growth and environmental pollution

Of these, deforestation is the most serious and the government has recently passed legislation to protect the country's remaining forests. This is because of the biodiversity of the forests. Moreover, the forests play a very important role globally in terms of the high levels of carbon dioxide they use.

Animals

Jaguars, boas, pelicans, otters, terns, manatees, marsh deer and pumas or cougars can all be found in Brazil.

Recreation

The national sport is soccer and Brazil has a very strong team. In fact, soccer is so important to them that businesses and schools may close when important international matches are played.

Basketball, volleyball, boating, swimming, fishing and motor racing are also all popular sports. The country went into mourning when Ayrton Senna, a Brazilian formula 1 driver was killed in 1994.

Additionally, going to the beach, socialising, dancing and listening to music are common pursuits.

Glossary

Import – products that the country buys from other countries.
Export – products that the country sells to other countries.
Biodiversity – the variety of plant species found in an area.

Comparison and contrast 1

Introducing the two items to be compared

An obvious similarity

Another obvious similarity

A less obvious similarity

An obvious difference

Another obvious difference

A less obvious difference

Overview

Conclusion

G6.2 Comparison and contrast 1

COMPARE	CONTRAST	OVERVIEW
similarly	as with	alternatively
equally	comparable to	by contrast
in the same way	however	whereas
likewise	but	on the other hand
compared with	generally	overall
unlike	on balance	ultimately

Comparison and contrast 2

Introducing the two items to be compared

↓

An obvious similarity

↓

Another obvious similarity

↓

A less obvious similarity

↓

An obvious difference

↓

Another obvious difference

↓

A less obvious difference

↓

Overview

↓

Conclusion

Section H: Pace and punch

H1.1 Short breathless sentences

Quick, hide!

Halt! Who goes there?

He spluttered, tripped and fell.

She stopped, stunned.

She opened the envelope and unfolded the letter she had dreaded which told her that it was all too late because Mr. Oldroyd was dead.

Alone, she wondered if anyone else had seen the creature and thought this was likely because the floodlights were shining on the trees and she could hear the beat of the music which meant there must be people nearby.

Tension

With one last desperate effort, Tom reached the alley. It was dark and deserted. His eyes swept round. On the ground lay the coat, crumpled. But before he could touch it, the siren wailed again. He stopped short. Lights flashed. He was trapped.

'You can't be serious,' Karen said. Her face shone in the torchlight. 'The path's too steep.'
'Scared?' Sharon sneered.
'No, but…'
'Then let's go,' Sharon added.
'Go?'
'Now!' Karen's voice echoed across the cave.
'I can't.'
'Or won't!'
Karen took the first step down the ladder.

Jo found himself on the edge of the cliff with no-one to guide him down. He could feel his heart pounding as fear took over every muscle and made him tremble and then left him unable to move. All of a sudden there was a sound below on the beach where he had seen the two men struggling over the boat.

H3.1 Long and easy sentences 1

From a tourist brochure:
Lounge in the long pool by the seashore and let your dreams come true.

Chocolate bar wrapper:
This chocolate is made for your delight and contains exotic fruits found only in Ethiopia, mountain mint made in Malaya and Turkish Delight from the Kalif's recipe in the palace at Ankora.

Book blurb:
Each book contains a special collection of eyewitness accounts and has been designed for you to enjoy as a single book, or as part of a special 10-book library.

Extract from a novel:
Entering the playground, Peter looked around, and to his surprise he saw John sitting ashen-faced in a distant corner.

An in-flight magazine:
Our modern airliners have a precise fix on location, can 'feel' their way around in bad weather and follow a programmed glide path to an automated landing.

Long and easy sentences 2

Peter walked across the playground. He was glad of the fresh air. The school looked bright in its new paint. He first saw Peter his friend in the corner. Then he saw Karen. Would Karen have the secret code?

Who could resist the chance of becoming a pop star? Certainly not David. However, he could not sing. He could not dance. He looked awkward when he walked. Everyone called him clumsy.

Travel through time with Wonder Time. It's the great new passport to the past, present and future. Visit the awesome Aztecs. See the chariots of Rome. Explore the Titanic. The tour starts here.

H5.1 Leaving the best till last

Magic trick:
Fill a glass with water. Place the coin in the glass of water. Stir three times. Say the magic word, 'Abracadabra'.
Hey Presto!
The coin disappears.

An advert:
As you move through the jungle, the prizes get bigger: you can win a CD; you can win a TV; you can win a DVD – you can even win a pot of gold!

Julius Caesar:
I came. I saw. I conquered.

Story:
As she took the spade, trowel and wheelbarrow to the bottom of the garden, the diamond ring fell from her pocket and into the long grass, where it stayed for 50 years.

Leaving the best till last

Joseph, known as the Treasure Finder, was an ace swimmer, but played hopelessly at football.

Sharon, who was a magician, disliked hockey and netball.

Charles Osborne, who hiccoughed for over 60 years, married twice, had eight children, was from Iowa, USA.

The Simpsons, the longest running series in the world, broadcast its 225th episode in 1999 and was created by Matt Groening.

We call them Celebrations: an assortment of milk chocolates, candied fruit and miniature biscuits.

H6.1 Paragraph endings 1

Jean-Marie Le Bris made and piloted two full-size gliders in the shape of sea birds. The gliders were masterpieces of engineering, and much admired. Le Bris based his first design on the aerodynamics of a large sea bird called an albatross, but unfortunately the glider did not fly like one. It crashed in the first thirty seconds.

The world's first steam train was built by Richard Trevithick. In 1804, it pulled carriages carrying 70 people a distance of 10 miles. It was an amazing start for one of history's most successful forms of transport.

'I'll just take the last rung of the ladder. The surface looks dusty. I'm stepping down. That's one small step for a man, one giant leap for mankind.'

Neil Armstrong as he stepped out to become the first man on the moon.

This started out as just a skive. And now look at us, lording it about in here. We'll be running the school soon. We already are......

Book blurb

Paragraph endings 2

Two weeks to Christmas:
We have become too busy! James was nearly caught, and that would have meant the end of our shelter. I can hardly remember ever going to bed. The shelter seems full of fruit cakes, pots of jam, Wellington boots and woolly jumpers to keep out the cold. James managed to bring torches for us all.

The invention of copper diving helmets in the 1800s meant that a diver could work nearly 200m below the surface. The helmet weighed about 9kg. You can try on a helmet in the diving display room. Open up, step inside and down you go. Fresh air was pumped down to the diver through a pipe. Modern armoured suits are worn by divers today.

Fire engines:
　　Loud siren
　　Flashing lights
　　Red and chrome body
　　Racing along – everyone turns to look
　　Telescopic ladder

H8.1) Paragraph rhythm 1

Join us with the tropical taste of new Rosatta refreshing drink. It sings. It celebrates. It refreshes. Take a long drink in a cool shade with Rosatta.

The castles of England tell their tales of knights, of chivalry, of life and death. See the Romans. Fight with the Vikings. Set sail for new lands. Walk the battlefields. Join them through a year's subscription to England's most popular History magazine, *Past Times*.

He waited by the corner for the rest of the gang. He knew. They all knew. Carter was finished, this time for good.

Quality time is precious. Relax in sumptuous shades of coral red amid luxurious layers of velvet cushions and chenille throws. You will find elegance. You will find indulgence. You will find yourself. Exclusively for everyone, designed for all: Treasure Interiors.

Paragraph rhythm 2

Extract from a magazine article
Get up to speed with the latest crash helmets.
They're safe. They're the ultimate. They're
roadworthy. They're chic. For those holding out
for top drawer labels, there's Gucci, Prada and
Dolce & Gabbana. Be the first in the market
place. There's plenty to choose from.

Film Star's comment:
'I want to be a star. The Oscar is the greatest
award in the world. To win! It's to have the
world fall in love with you. It's a dream come
true. Anything can happen.'

Football commentary.
It's Stevens on the left with an opening now,
with an opening to Bell on the inside. Can he
see it? Can he? He's got to act fast. He can't
keep it to himself much longer. He challenges.
He goes. There's the move!

H9.2 Paragraph rhythm 2

Tourist advert

Come to Discovery Cove. There are no barriers, no cares and no crowds. Just make a reservation and arrive. Imagine spending a holiday with your family in an exclusive oasis. Think of swimming with dolphins in the ocean. Dream of gliding among the waterfalls. Do all these things at Discovery Cove.

Extract from a story:

The end of term was a succession of cold wet days. Football had begun and Peter was pleased to be in the team. He played in defence, he played in goal. He also played in the forwards, and he played on the wing. By the time Christmas came, he had played everywhere on the field. It rained continually until the holidays.

Section I: Standard English

I1.1 # Great things about writing

A well it wasn't really a holiday more a ...an expedition

B why did you?

A oh I guess because we ed- we ended up carrying so much equipment and

C that sounds like a trip I took....um....two years ago I think...Yeah in the summer and I've never gone again

---

BRITON, 22, DIES ON MONT BLANC

A British climber fell 2,000 feet to his death as he was descending Mont Blanc. The Briton, aged 22, is believed to have slipped as he tried to run the last few yards over a dangerous gully.

Great things about writing

A

It was years before Christopher Chant told anyone about his dreams. This was because he mostly lived in the nursery at the top of the big London house, and the nursery maids who looked after him changed every few months.

The Lives of Christopher Chant, Diane Wynne Jones

B

There were four gangs at our school. Four real gangs. Lots of the juniors made up pretend gangs and went round boasting about it, but we just ignored them. We seniors knew about gangs and that's why there were only four – one for each year of the seniors. Everyone wanted to be in their year gang – it was the best thing that could happen to you. Sometimes you'd laugh at them and say you didn't care. But that was just to make out you couldn't be bothered. All the time everyone was dying to be a gang member. I certainly was.

The Ceremony, Martin Copus

12.1 **Great things about speech**

Conversation at the bus stop.

A I knew something was wrong when

B   yes

A because the back door was sh- shut

B aye

A back door shut and and the dog how-, er howling. I could hear it from the street

B so weren't you frightened?

A didn't think
c- crossed my mind later like that er there might have been someone inside the h- house.

Cricket commentary:

McKenzie comes in
bowls
and Barrington makes a most ungraceful little jab there to a ball that goes through to Grout.

McKenzie scrubs it furiously on his flannels and starts off on that rather buoyant bouncing run of his.

Great things about speech

No go.

You're welcome.

Eight?

Four spades.

Reach.

M'lud.

No, rare.

Try.

In-off again.

13.1

Appropriateness in speech and writing 1

Well, it was dark, see. This boy was walking home and he was going across this wood and it was late and he was getting cold and he wanted to get home as quick as he could. Well, it was really late and everything, and he got scared 'cos he'd heard of really creepy things happening in these woods. Then he hears this noise.

Appropriateness in speech and writing 2

Scientists have reported a remarkable step forward for mankind this week.

In a valley in East Africa last Friday morning, it was reported that a hominid by the name of Fred walked upright on two legs rather than four.

It happened here, at about 2pm last Sunday.

The local news agency is hailing the walk as "One small step for a man, one giant leap for hominid-kind."

MAN WALKS!!!!

I'm here in the rift valley looking over the rocky terrain where Zog was first discovered.

We'll bring you more news as it comes in.

Zog claims to have trained on wild berries and honey for the stupendous achievement.

14.2

Appropriateness in speech and writing 2

The hormones make the adrenal glands stimulate neurons of the hypothalamus and of the reticular formations.

Hand gumming can rarely be done with an ordinary shovel.

Capped fuses have the advantage of showing an efficient and waterproof crimp.

Some are hailing it as the most spectacular event of the age.

Agreement

When they get to the beach, they tied up the horse and made sandcastles which was later wash away by the sea. Then Jenny says, 'What are that by the rock near the edge of the water?'

I6.1 Formality 1

Formal
Excuse me, but could you lend me a pen, please?

Less formal
Have you got a pen I can borrow, please?

Informal
Have you got a pen?

Thank you for not smoking

No smoking

Please do not smoke

Ask someone to be quiet

Invite someone to a party

Request that someone get out of the way

Formality 2

Rules for visiting football fans:

- No running onto the pitch

- No throwing onto the pitch

- Do Not Enter This Area

- Take Your Litter With You When You Leave

I7.2 Formality 2

A magazine editorial

Hi! Welcome to a very special issue of EVERYONE, edited by Sue, Tina, Gary and Vince and Jack the terrier. No, only joking – Jack joined us in the editing room, but we did all the work!

This week we have a fabulous galaxy of new stories, along with the best in the pop world, sport and top fashion. We ask the tough questions of tough athletes.

While the girls were tackling their mammoth sports task, the boys were deciding this week's fashion news.

Hey, why not join them? OK?

Information article

More than 300 plants usually found in tropical rainforests have just taken root in the world's largest greenhouse, found in St Blazy, Cornwall.

The greenhouse, or biome, is part of the Eden project that opened to the public this spring, where visitors can see more than 12,000 plants and trees from all over the world.

Among the more unusual species planted is the Cananga Odorata from Malaysia which is used to make posh French perfume, Chanel No 5!

Rules for a competition

Play your Part.
It's the biggest competition in the UK.
To enter, tell us the highest mountain in the world. Send a postcard to the address on page 16. Mark your entry *Play Your Part*. Remember to include your name, age and address. Your entry must arrive no later than December 2nd.

Formality 3

Three cheers for the team. Hip hip, hooray!

Happy birthday!

I pronounce you man and wife.

Please give generously to the Save the Children Fund.

DO NOT WALK ON THE GRASS

Trespassers will be prosecuted.

Danger. 5000 Volts.

Please leave in an orderly fashion.

Silence in court

Put your specs on, ref!

18.2

Formality 3

Wonka Xploder tongue-crackling chocolate.

Dinosaur mug promotion:
Win a free dinosaur mug
Make drink time fun with our Limited Edition Dinosaur mug. There are two designs to collect, Aladar and Neera. Each ceramic mug has a colourful funky design.

Consumer information:
Nestles Consumer Services
The Willy Wonka Candy Factory
PO Box No 203
York Y09 1XY

Best before information:
See under seal.

Ingredients:
Milk chocolate, Sugar, Crisped rice, Lactose, Vegetable fat, Glucose syrup, Carbon dioxide. May contain nut traces.

Section J: Other types of non-fiction

J1.1 Text types 1

Instruction

Explanation

Recount

Information

Persuasion

Discursive writing

Analysis

Evaluation

Text types 1

A Generally, the group worked quite well together, but...

B This is because...

C During the winter there is competition for food and therefore...

D When we went on our trip to...

E The use of repetition reinforces an impression of...

F The environment at this latitude is...

G How a bird flies

H On the other hand, there is partial evidence of...

I Next, apply the glue to the base of the leg.

J Buy now!

K Help bring cheer to old people's lives today.

L Whereas some countries have legalised the drug, many still consider it a danger.

M I think that our design would have been more successful if we had used a stronger material to cover the wings.

N Twenty years earlier...

O Finally, serve warm with a side salad.

P The implication is that...

J2.1 Text types 2

Instructions	• Use of imperative verbs, starts with a command • Use of sequencing connectives e.g. next, finally • Simple direct language for ease of use on the job
Explanation	• Impersonal & formal • Present tense • Formal or technical vocabulary
Recount	• Use of past tense • Use of 'I' and 'We' suggests personal recount • Use of temporal connectives e.g. earlier, when
Information	• Impersonal & formal • Present tense • Formal or technical vocabulary
Persuasion	• Direct address to reader • Emotive language e.g. cheer • Urgent language e.g. use of exclamation mark
Discursive writing	• Connectives for contrast e.g. whereas, on the other hand • Terms of qualification e.g. some countries, partial evidence • Balanced sentence structures e.g. Whereas some… many still…
Analysis	• Vocabulary of analysis and justification e.g. implication, effective because • Impersonal to imply impartial analysis • Present tense
Evaluation	• Use of qualifications e.g. Generally, quite, but • Direct judgements e.g. quite well, successful • Use of conditionals e.g. would have been

Text types 2

Giving directions to get from one place to another	A recipe
How hydro-electric power is generated	The life cycle of the frog
Witness statement to police	Match report
Entry in an encyclopaedia	A leaflet explaining Christmas opening hours at a shopping centre
An election manifesto	A charity appeal
An essay about the pros and cons of wind-powered electricity	A magazine article about the issues surrounding the privacy of royal children
A poetry appreciation	A commentary which interprets a set of statistical data
Commentary on the successes and limitations of a product and what might be improved	A self-assessment of one's work over the term

J4.1 Text types 4

Consider the facts…

We were successful in…

Although the battle had been won…

There are several reasons…

When you reach this stage…

Next…

The evidence suggests…

Can you imagine…?

_____ is an interesting character because…

Perhaps the most significant reason was…

Adaptations

In conclusion…

The quotation reveals…

When your diagram is complete…

Mix carefully

I am pleased with…

When we first arrived…

_____ is a controversial topic because…

Later…

There are opposing views concerning…

Evidence suggests that…

Perhaps a target for future assessments could be…

The life-cycle of…

To light a gas lamp…

Ever since then…

Habitat and Food

Take the saw and…

Although…

Therefore…

Sun, sea and sand

Picture this…

A major factor contributing to…

I could have…

My aim next time is to…

In the year 2001…

Giving directions

It's easy. You come out of the bus station and go down the road, then you turn right. There's some traffic lights and a roundabout. It's down there and it's along a bit. Just a two minute walk. It's on the right up there. There's a shopping centre. You can see it once you're there.

Turn left out of the main exit from the bus station.

Walk down Smith Street, past the Post Office on your left.

Then, at the traffic lights, turn right into Church Street.

Continue down Church Street until you reach the mini-roundabout, then turn right into Smith Place.

The office will be directly ahead of you, opposite the shopping centre.

J6.1 Instructions

HOW TO REVISE

A Have a short break and then later ask someone to test you orally, or test yourself.

B After this, summarise the information, using key words only.

C Re-read the relevant sections of your notes, underlining key ideas.

D Collate all your materials in the place where you will be working (preferably at your desk).

E Finally, have a good night's sleep, so that you are fresh and able to give your best in your test the next day!

F Next, check your answers to see what sections of the work you need to go over in more detail.

G Ensure you know what sections of your work need to be studied.

H Next, change the form of your notes. For example, you could draw a flow-chart, use colours to create a mind map, think of a mnemonic, or present the information in a table or chart.

I Then, use the key words to rewrite full sentences with detailed information about your topic.

Explanation

A

Several species are threatened with extinction, and the main reason is man's greed and cruelty. Elephants, for example, are hacked to death by poachers who sell their tusks for ivory. The same fate befalls rhinoceroses. This horrible cruelty must be stopped!

B

Several species are threatened with extinction. Examples are elephants, rhinoceroses, wild birds, snakes, dolphins, whales, tigers, leopards, cheetahs and wild dogs. As numbers dwindle, the need to protect and provide for their needs is urgent.

C

Several species are threatened with extinction because of loss of territory. Natural habits are eroded by the growth of towns and cities and by the pollution that comes with them. The forests and jungles are redeveloped for farming, industry and residential space. Food sources thus disappear and the animals are forced to move to other less suitable habitats. There, they often fail to thrive, and sometimes they develop illnesses as a result of pollution in the rivers and atmosphere.

J7.2 Explanations

- The problem or issue is explained, with reasons

- Active verbs

- Present tense

- Third person

- Cause and effect connectives: *as a result*, *therefore*, *because*, etc

- Sequence or time connectives: *first*, *next*, *finally*, etc

- Paragraphs are used to introduce different reasons

- A number of reasons for an event or process is given

- Specialised vocabulary may be used

- Focus is on factual detail, not emotive language

Recount

Conflict flared at last night's third round play-off between Spurs and Arsenal.

Supporters clashed after a player was sent off for aggressive tackling. Ironically, the same player had been the victim of several controversial tackles earlier in the game, none of which had been followed up by the referee. Consequently, there had been strong criticism of the referee even before the incident took place.

Abusive and unruly behaviour on the terraces led to an early end to the first half, at which point several spectators were escorted from the ground.

Fights developed later between rival supporters, resulting in several arrests. One man was taken to hospital with a knife wound.

J8.2 Recount

- Start with establishing overview of the event

- Sequenced in order of event

- Paragraphed by phase of action or event

- Several connectives to signal time passing e.g. later

- Use of past tense

- Usually written impersonally in third person

- Use of active voice, so it's clear who did what

- Several connectives indicate cause and effect e.g. resulting in

- Factual coverage rather than direct expression of opinion

- Other people's opinions reported but not necessarily endorsed

- Avoidance of biased language

Persuasion

The flat was too small to swing a cat. So it was kicked, punched and burned instead.

When the vet inspected Raquel the cat, he noted a fractured leg, broken ribs, blood swelling to the head and a ruptured abdomen.

The kind of injuries consistent with a road accident. Except this cat had never left her owner's flat.

You see, it wasn't a speeding vehicle that had struck her. It was a boot.

The rest of her injuries revealed a sad catalogue of suffering.

Severe burns. Scald lesions. Broken and fractured bones. Ruptures. Haematoma. Chronic arthritis caused by a fractured hock.

The owner assumed that Raquel, used to living in large houses, had incurred these injuries running around her cramped flat.

The owner's boyfriend, who was found guilty of the horrific accidents, was then sentenced to three months in an extremely cramped place of his own.

Last year, our inspectors investigated over 124,000 cruelty complaints. Thankfully, this one had a happy ending.

Under the RSPCA's care, Raquel made a good recovery and is now re-homed in a loving environment. She remains scared of men but is making steady progress.

RSPCA week runs until 25th April. Please join, support us or make a donation by calling 01403 223 284 during office hours.

Despite our best efforts, cruelty to cats is creeping up every year. But with your help, we are determined to reverse this trend.

J9.2 Persuasion

Powerful opening statement to catch attention

Emotive language to stimulate a sympathetic reaction

Use of bold and varied font sizes to gain attention

Humour to get the reader on the writer's side or make them think

Imperatives (commands) which tell the reader what to do

Short sentences for a blunt, dramatic effect and to keep interest

Alliteration so words and ideas are remembered

Addresses reader directly

Personal and informal tone to suggest like-mindedness

Use of contrasts to emphasise particular points

Use of facts to shock the reader

Shock tactics

Analysis

Throughout the poem the various moods of the sea are compared to those of a dog. This unusual comparison provides some startling but effective imagery. 'With his clashing teeth and shaggy jaws' evokes the noise and movement of the sea in a storm, developing the visual image introduced in line 2 of the 'grey' scene, reflecting the colour of the storm clouds. Similarly, the use of 'moans' suggests pain. The whole stanza is very active, with all the verbs revealing the restless nature of the sea.

The survey reveals that the majority of purchases are made by females between the ages of 25-50, but that of these 80% are in the 40-45 age group. This group are also the biggest spenders, particularly in the purchase of trainers and sweatshirts. Their average expenditure per visit is £35. Curiously, their purchases are rarely made for themselves but for teenagers. The statistics prove that when it comes to sports fashions, Mum still holds the purse strings.

J10.2 Analysis

The poem, 'The Sea', by James Reeves described how the sea is like a dog. The poet described the sea: 'rolls on the beach all day'. He also said the sea 'moans'.

In the second stanza the sea 'howls' and shakes his wet fur over the cliffs, which I thought was very good. It changed the feeling of the poem.

In the end he writes about the sea sleeping quietly. I think this is when it's calm, like when the dog snores quietly. The poem is very effective.